RECRUITER SECRETS

Insider Tips for Your **Job Search**

ERIC R. DERBY, SPHR

DERBY PUBLISHING

Recruiter Secrets: Insider Tips for Your Job Search

While every precaution has been taken in the preparation of this book, the author and publisher assume no responsibility for errors or omissions, or for damages resulting from the use of the information contained herein.

Copyright © 2021 Eric R. Derby.

All rights reserved. Except as permitted under U.S. Copyright Act of 1976, no part of this publication may be reproduced, distributed, or transmitted in any form or by any means, or stored in a database or retrieval system, without the prior written permission of the publisher.

   Published by Derby Publishing.

ISBN: 978-17364306-1-3

Written by Eric R. Derby.

Cover, logo, and internal design by Rachael T. Derby.

First edition. January 26, 2021.

RECRUITER SECRETS

🔍 TABLE OF CONTENTS

FORWARD: By Hannah Morgan, Career Sherpa 1

PREFACE 3

CHAPTER ONE: The Preliminaries 5
- Why I wrote this book 5
- My inspiration for the title 5
- Contrarian 6
- Whom is this book for? 6
- Biases and disclaimers 7
- My history 8
- How to use this book 8

CHAPTER TWO: For the Unemployed 9
- Grief 9
- Getting laid off 10
- Getting fired 10
- Bad employer, harassment, etc. 11
- Job as identity 12
- Balance 13
- Allies 13
- Additional sources 14
- Survival jobs 15

CHAPTER THREE: For the Employed 17
- Why are you looking? 17
- If you are just looking for a raise 18
- Improving compensation 19
- Frequency of job change 20
- Reduced working hours 20
- Moving up 21

CHAPTER FOUR: Self-Assessment 23
- You were not trained for this 23
- The mind resists change 23
- The ideal job 24
- Know yourself 25
- Shaman's death 25
- Why are you on this planet? 26
- What is your passion? 27
- What is great about you? 28
- Changing careers 28
- Persistence 29
- Career coach 30

CHAPTER FIVE: Prepare 33
- General 33
- Set goals 33
- Track job search activity 34
- Elevator pitch 35
- Business cards? 36
- Know your market value 36
- About references 38
- Getting references 39

CHAPTER SIX: Career Marketing Plan 41
- What is a career marketing plan? 41
- Elements or sections 42

CHAPTER SEVEN: Cover Letters 45
- Do you need a cover letter? 45
- What is in a good cover letter? 46
- Alternate cover letter 47

CHAPTER EIGHT: All About Résumés 49
- Overview 49
- Contrarian views 50
- How recruiters read résumés 50
- Slogging through résumés 51
- Visual perspective 52
- Three green lights 52
- You are not your résumé 53
- You are the product 54
- Résumé vs. CV 54
- Types of résumés 55
- Résumé writers 56

CHAPTER NINE: Making Your Résumé 57
- Résumé basics 57
- Blocks of text 58
- Name and contact information 59
- Sections 59
- Brain stuff 60
- Objective 61
- Alternative Objective 62
- Skills Overview 62
- Tables (making data visually available) 63
- Formatting Work Experience 64
- Accomplishments (by the numbers) 65
- Accomplishments (hooks or loops) 65
- Keywords 66
- Show growth patterns 67
- Résumé gaps 67

- Résumés and discrimination 68
- Personal information 69
- Awards, Education, final notes 70

CHAPTER TEN: HR and How Companies Work 73
- A day in the life of an HR person 73
- How to annoy a recruiter 74
- Not our job 75
- Priority of recruiting 75
- Hiring process 76
- Finding a contact in a company 77
- Broken hiring process 78

CHAPTER ELEVEN: The Search 81
- Discrimination in your job search? Just move on. 81
- Respect 81
- Finding jobs (overview) 82
- Groups (more ways to find jobs) 83
- Job boards and job aggregators, oh my 84
- Search agents 85
- Posted job requirements 86
- Bad job postings 87
- Applying online 88
- Different ways to apply 89
- Stopping by to apply 89
- Internal referrals 90
- Posting your résumé 91
- What is an ATS? 92
- ATS problems 93
- Social media 94

- Branding 95
- The black hole 96
- Following up to an application 97
- Effective emails 98
- Personality tests 99
- Freelance work 100
- It may not be there 101

CHAPTER TWELVE: Networking 103
- Informational interviews 103
- Networking: still the best way 104
- Under-used alumni 105
- Networking events 106
- Career fairs 107
- LinkedIn 108
- LinkedIn profile 110

CHAPTER THIRTEEN: Working with a Third-party Recruiter 113
- Definitions 113
- Agency methods 113
- Agency recruiters 114
- How to find an agency 115
- How to work with a third-party recruiter 116
- Pros of working with a third-party recruiter 118
- Cons of working with a third-party recruiter 118
- Agencies and résumés 119
- Headhunters 120
- Placement agent 121
- Candidate control 121

CHAPTER FOURTEEN: Interview Preparation 123
- Interview overview 123
- Interview process 124
- Interview schedule 125
- Researching the job and company 126
- Interview your manager 127
- Talk with a peer 128
- Dress code 129
- Tattoos and piercings 129
- Common questions asked 130
- Questions that everyone hates 131
- Storytelling 133
- Standing out from the crowd 134

CHAPTER FIFTEEN: The Interview 135
- Everything is important 135
- Be yourself 136
- First 10 seconds 136
- Parents 137
- Phone 137
- BYOD? 138
- Bad interviewer 139
- Negativity 139
- How people get hired 140
- More on rapport 141
- Tests 142
- What if I do not like it? 143
- Determine cultural fit 144
- Legal salary discussions 145

- Better salary discussions 146
- Have questions 147
- Asking for feedback 148
- Ask for what is next 149

CHAPTER SIXTEEN: Remote Interviews 151
- Phone interviews 151
- Video interviews 152

CHAPTER SEVENTEEN: Closing the Deal 155
- Changing job descriptions 155
- Thank-you notes 155
- Follow up, patience 156
- Social media checks 157
- Limbo 158
- Second chances 159
- Getting feedback, Part II 159
- Dealing with rejection 161
- Job offers in writing 161
- Basis for salary 162
- Low-ball salary companies 163
- Delay tactics 164
- Counteroffers from you 165
- It is OK to say no 166
- Reviewing your goals 166
- Deciding and accepting 167
- Resignation letter 168
- Counteroffers from your employer 169
- Exit interviews 170

CHAPTER EIGHTEEN: A New Beginning **171**
- Starting a new job 171
- Forward networking 171
- If it does not work out 172
- Keep a résumé ready 173
- Keeping up with the job market 173

CHAPTER NINETEEN: Coronavirus Update **175**
- SARS-CoV-2, Covid-19, Coronavirus 175
- What to do differently 175
- Hiring process changes 177
- Work changes 178

CHAPTER TWENTY: The End **179**
- Thank you 179

FORWARD: By Hannah Morgan, Career Sherpa

Wouldn't you love to get inside the head of a recruiter to understand how candidates are evaluated and who gets forwarded along to hiring managers?

This is exactly the information Eric Derby, an independent recruiter with 20 plus years of experience, encapsulated in this book. He doesn't hold back. Derby recounts stories of successful and not-so-successful job seekers he's encountered. He offers advice, warnings and motivation to help employed and unemployed job seekers.

This book is especially helpful for the millions who have suddenly found themselves laid off in the pandemic and who are trying to navigate a job search during uncertain times. Job seekers need an ally and honest advice from someone who has counseled thousands of candidates over his career.

I met Eric Derby during the Great Recession and I respected and valued his perspective then and still do today! It isn't enough to throw your résumé at job postings. It takes more work than that. "Recruiter Secrets" delivers answers to many questions job seekers have—and even answers questions they didn't know to ask.

Hannah Morgan
Founder, Job Search Strategist
CareerSherpa.net

PREFACE

The Novel Coronavirus, also known as SARS-CoV-2 and Covid-19, is causing massive changes in the working world. If it wasn't already difficult finding a new job, the pandemic made it tougher.

The good news is that most aspects of looking for a new job have not changed. As such, I have not made any modifications to most of the chapters, and have instead added Chapter Nineteen to discuss the changes in the process.

In any case, the pandemic only increased the need for job seekers to arm themselves with as much helpful information as possible, including the tips and advice contained in this book.

CHAPTER ONE: The Preliminaries

Why I wrote this book

I have been a recruiter since 1998. Over those 22 years I would like to think that I have learned a few useful things about helping people find jobs. I want to share these things and help people along on their journey. While I get paid to help companies find the right talent, I find that I am regularly coaching people about their job search. Sometimes I provide free workshops like "The Visual Résumé" or "Networking for Introverts," but most of the time I am providing people with information over the phone or writing on-line responses.

Recently I found myself responding to a post by a person who was having a tough time in a job search. I realized as I was writing that I was repeating myself. I had written, or spoken, much the same advice enough times that I had lost count.

I was struck by the idea that I should write a book. What a wonderful way to help even more people without repeating myself. Additionally, I could become a better and more efficient, teacher.

So here it is.

My inspiration for the title

Several years ago, I heard about a speaker coming to Rochester, New York. She was on a mission to help a million job seekers. She went by the name Absolutely Abby (www.absolutelyabby.com) and I went to see a few of her presentations. She had a set of well-organized presentations and was very well-informed on job-search topics. I realized that I already knew most of what she was telling people. I could have been the one at the front of the room speaking.

That motivated me to launch a local speaker panel called "Recruiter Secrets." A panel was arranged to get local recruiters to talk about their thoughts and tell job seekers how things really worked to help more people find employment.

It turned out to be a successful panel.

I had come up with the title based on many articles I had read that detailed the secrets of many professions. With Abby's inspiration the title was born. It made sense to me when I started to write this book that I should use that same title.

Contrarian

I am not a typical recruiter. I have plenty of references, both candidates and employer clients, who would tell you that. My methods are different from those of other recruiters or agencies in a variety of ways, starting with an unusual business model for my company. I like to be innovative and improve old techniques. I prefer to talk with fewer people and have deeper conversations. I like to help people find the right job. I could make more money if I wanted to follow traditional agency models. But I am more motivated by helping people.

Or maybe I just do things differently because it got boring doing the same thing that all the other agencies are doing.

As you read through this book, you will find ideas that are far from normal practice. You will find suggestions that are the opposite of what other recruiters and agencies might suggest. Some may make sense. Others may be counterintuitive. Some may get my competitors mad at me.

I am not saying that all my ideas are different and radical. Many follow more traditional wisdom, but with my own special slant. You can expect me to tell you things that others are unlikely to. I hope I surprise you.

I encourage you to try things. See what works. If something I wrote works for you, that is wonderful. If not, just move on. I do not expect that everything I write here will work for everyone. I hope that these ideas will help you find a job that will allow you to wake up with more enthusiasm every day.

Whom is this book for?

Obviously, it's for job seekers trying to land the right position. Many people are working at jobs that are boring, unfulfilling or repetitive. Each person desires that ideal job that will fire their imagination and adrenaline at the same time. But they have little idea where to begin.

Part of my goal is not just to help find your next position, but also to help you find the best imaginable job for you.

As people change, their goals and job objectives evolve. What may have been the perfect job for you a few years ago may not be the right one now. And that perfect job now may not be perfect a decade down the road. You will continue to grow and change and need something new. This is the new normal because we live in a culture that is constantly changing.

Whether you are employed or unemployed, I am going to help you find that next great position. One section of the book is specifically for those who are currently employed, and another section is for those who are unemployed.

Most sections of the book are for all job seekers.

Biases and disclaimers

My background differs from most recruiters. The ideas described in this book may not fit all professions, though I have tried to make them generic.

I want to let you know my biases upfront.

I am an independent person and have been self-employed for most of my career.

I wrote an ethics policy, even though I am a one-person company. I believe in doing things the right way. I will not serve a client company that is unethical or that treats their employees poorly. I have dropped clients for these reasons.

I am an introvert. You probably find that strange for a recruiter. I have developed a business model that works well for myself. I make fewer calls, but spend more time on each call. I dislike making cold calls. Some topics in this book are from an introvert's perspective. Not to worry. I am confident an extrovert can adapt to those few items.

I have a technical background. Most of my recruiting work has been filling technical positions. You may see that some of my examples and stories are about technical people.

In the pages ahead, I am offering topics and ideas to help you get a great and fulfilling job. But the bottom line is that you are responsible for your job search and career. Take the topics here as input and, within ethical guidelines, make your own best decisions about your work life.

My history

I have a Bachelor of Science degree in Computer Science from Rochester Institute of Technology.

I was a software developer for seven years. I was laid off.

I found a job as a network manager. I was laid off and accidentally found a job as a recruiter. I worked for a small private direct-placement agency. When the owner retired, I went out on my own. I did quite well for a few years.

In the tough years after the 2000-2002 dot-com crash, I started a business repairing computers and ran that for several years.

I found a position working as an account manager (sales, really) for a large staffing agency. I was not happy and started looking for a new position. They found out and fired me immediately. I found a new position working for a different agency. I started out as a recruiter and worked at what is called a blended desk (both sales and recruiting).

I restarted my own company with an unusual business model in 2007. I have been running my company with that model since then.

Overall, I have experienced many of the same events, like layoffs, that other job seekers have experienced. They've helped me better understand and work with candidates.

How to use this book

I have written this so that it can be used as a reference book.

Originally each topic was one page long. But I found that e-books have fewer words per page, and I could not fit most topics onto a single page. Topics will be covered in one to two pages.

Complex topics have been broken down into smaller topics, and topics have been grouped together in chapters.

You can read it all the way through, or just go to the chapters or topics that you need, as you need them.

If you are not employed, I would suggest at least skimming the book all the way through. The job search process can be long and complicated. Being aware of the problems and pitfalls of a search before they happen can make you more resilient when problems occur.

Because of the way the topics are broken down, you can read one or two at a time, between other projects or while waiting in a lobby for an interview, for example. Whatever works for you.

CHAPTER TWO: For the Unemployed

Grief

I had a phone call with Jim after he had the on-site interview with my client. He knew that it had not gone well. All through the interview, he kept thinking about his old job and how things were done there. He was slow to respond and did not answer some questions well. It was unfortunate. I knew from my original phone interview with him that he could succeed at that job. He was not yet over losing the old job, which caused him to perform poorly at the on-site interview.

Losing your job can be hard. Many people's identity is directly tied to the work they do. If you lost your job, you might feel as if you have lost a part of yourself. And you have. You lose the sense of purpose that you got from your job.

You lose the income. If you earn the primary income for your family, that can be significantly more stressful. You may have difficulty paying rent or a mortgage, keeping insurance policies going, making car payments and paying phone bills.

Your family might be affected. You may have to cancel a vacation or may not have money to assist a child with college tuition.

Some people can put their grief on a shelf. Others need to deal with it before they can move on. Most people will have to deal with the loss while moving on.

Get help. Talk with friends. Talk with a counselor. If you cannot afford a counselor, talk with a minister, priest or rabbi.

You must deal with this.

If you go into an interview and have not dealt with your grief, or at least started to, that will affect your interview performance. I am not saying that your grieving has to be completed, but you cannot let it dominate your life — or your interview.

I have seen people fail interviews because of this. It is almost painful to interview people like this. They cannot do the job they are seeking, even if it is similar to what they have done previously. Even if I know they could have been great at it.

To go into an interview and look forward to new work you must work on your grieving.

I could say the same things about anger.

Getting laid off

It happens to many people. Often.

Fortunately, getting laid off does not have the stigma that it once had. In the past it was often seen as a sign that you were not a good worker or that you had another problem.

I have been laid off twice myself. You could say that I was lucky or you could say that I found some positives in an unpleasant situation.

The first time, I was working as a software developer.

- I was able to start my job search several weeks before the old job ended, with the knowledge of the employer, which made it much easier.
- I could tell people I was a valued employee. I was hired as No. 32 in the department and laid off as No. 19. I made it through several layoffs.
- I was able to finish my project ahead of schedule. While this caused the layoff to come earlier than planned and reduced my pay, I was able to use that to sell my work ethic to potential employers.

The second time I was laid off, I was working as a network administrator at a university, which lost the grant that funded my job.

After that job I found my way into recruiting.

My point here is that getting laid off is not the end of the world.

Some thoughts:

- Do not advertise the layoff on your résumé. If someone asks why the job ended, tell them the truth. If you know the reason, then you can explain the layoff. Tell interviewers how many other people were laid off as well.
- Look for positives. What do you want that will be better in the next job?

Getting fired

I was fired from a job once.

I was working for a staffing agency. I was not happy with the job or the company, so I started to look for a new job. The company found out about it and fired me immediately. This is common in staffing agencies, because they think that their customer data will be stolen.

In my case it is easy to tell people about how and why I got fired. It has never had a detrimental impact on my career.

I do not expect that this would be the case for most people. Getting fired will generally make your job search tougher.

Should you tell people why you were fired? I cannot give you an answer, because it would depend on too many things. I would say that in most cases it is probably better not to say, or provide only general information. It is acceptable to decline providing more information. Understand that it may annoy the interviewer and that you have to move past that. Do not lie about being fired.

If you were fired for doing something illegal, it will be discovered in a background check. Don't hide that you were fired; just avoid details, such as office politics. Talking about the details will not help.

The key here is to show how you have moved on and how you have improved since then. Getting fired does not have to kill an interview if you can show that you have learned and that you are better because of it.

What if you have not changed or improved? Fix it. Change. Improve. If possible, demonstrate how you have changed. You do not have a choice if you want a better job.

Bad employer, harassment, etc.

If your previous employment ended because of a bad work environment, harassment or discrimination, it is best not to talk about those things to a potential employer. Talk with friends, a therapist or an attorney, but do not talk about it in a professional setting, be it an interview or even a networking event.

It is likely that you will be asked about your previous employer in an interview. Stay focused on the positive, the things you liked and the things you accomplished.

Negative things can destroy an interview very quickly.

Do not speak poorly of your previous employer.

These things will portray you as a negative person, and they will not hire you. I have seen many excellent candidates get rejected because they spoke negatively of a previous employer. In this case the truth does not matter. Giving a negative but accurate portrayal of your previous employer will not help you get the job.

What should you say? Keep it very general. i.e., "There was an internal conflict." The less you say the better. "We had a disagreement on the direction and responsibilities of the position." If the interviewer presses, you can always say that it is confidential. In the case of harassment, your attorney probably asked you not to talk about it. Again, keep it general like, "I agreed not to discuss the details," rather than, "My attorney told me not to talk about it."

Focus on what you want in the new position, i.e., you want management that is transparent; you want a position with a good work-life balance, a place where employees are respected, etc. In short, keep it positive and work-based and avoid personal disagreements and entanglements.

Job as identity

Our careers take up the greatest portion of our lives. Most people spend more time at their jobs than they spend with their families.

That makes it hard not to at least partly identify with your job. I have found this to be true more for men than women. Men can be hit harder emotionally when they lose their jobs.

Think about going to a party. What are the most common discussions when people meet for the first time? "What do you do?" "Where do you work?"

This makes for a black-and-blue mark on the ego when a job is lost.

But you are not your job.

Use that as a meditation mantra. Talk with friends, counselors, career coaches. Think and talk about who you are beyond your job.

I am not trying to be a pop psychologist here. This is practical information.

If your sense of self is cracked, get some super glue or duct tape and get yourself back together. If you do not, those cracks will be apparent in an interview and can cause you to do poorly and not get the job.

Balance

Being unemployed is hard. It is hard to find a balance between taking care of yourself and looking for the next job.

Doing a job search is hard, tedious work most of us weren't trained for. Very few people can spend all day, five days a week, doing it. Not only are a limited number of positions available at any given time, also, in most cases, it involves a lot of waiting and tedium.

Try to create a balance. Take care of yourself by finding time to do something that relaxes you. Take time to be with family, to visit friends, to work on projects that have been ignored. Read for pleasure or try something new.

In a work-related vein, call or email people in your network or get together for lunch with previous coworkers.

Few people are going to find a new job in a couple of weeks. Do not stress yourself trying to do the impossible.

Take time to think about what you really want. After all, this might be the right time to make the change that you have been dreaming about.

Find balance.

Allies

You cannot do it alone. Maybe a few people can do it alone.

Most can't. I can't. Don't be the Lone Ranger. Our culture says that you need to be strong, independent and self-sufficient. As if you did not already have enough pressure.

Get support. Talk to people.

You are not alone in this. You are far from the first person to be unemployed. Odds are that you know a few others who are also unemployed. Or have friends who were unemployed.

People get laid off every day. Every month more than 1 percent of the current workforce gets laid off, according to the U.S. Bureau of Labor Statistics.

You are not alone.

Get help by networking. Join a job-search group.

The highest percentage of jobs are still found through networking, so finding people to help is the single best thing you can do to help your search.

Stay connected by asking for help. And be willing to help others.

Additional sources

If unemployed, you have many resources for help.

For example, outsourcing services:

Some people get referred to outsourcing services when they are laid off. If you are offered a service like this, use it! Those that I have known are very good. They are staffed by people who really want to help you find your next job. The experience of the workers is generally varied, so no matter what your need, they probably have someone who can help.

They often have job-search support groups, individual coaching, help with résumés, job-search tools and so much more.

Some of these companies now offer their services remotely. I do not yet have much feedback on this, but I personally would not like it as much if I was meeting people only virtually. If that is all you have, take advantage of it; it will still be better than no help at all.

Unemployment and workforce-development offices:

These go by many names depending on where you live. But they are basically state or federally funded programs to help people find work. Services and quality vary, but it is always worth checking out what is available.

Some states have special programs where you can continue to collect unemployment checks while starting a business. Typically, it is hard to get into one of these programs, but if you have always wanted to start a business, this might be a way to do it.

Get help wherever it is offered. You can never tell where you might find the lead to your next great job.

Survival jobs

There are many times in my life that I have been accused of being an optimist. Often this was not meant in a positive way. It was implied that I was not being realistic.

I dream big. That is part of what motivates me. That is part of what gives me my drive and energy and enthusiasm.

You may read what I wrote and think that it is not possible. That finding a better job will not happen.

I am not saying that it is easy. It is a lot of hard work. It is work that may never end. You may always be looking for a better job.

But sometimes necessity is more important than dreams.

You may need to take a job to pay bills; to feed the family and pay the rent. It may seem that all of your time is taken up in just surviving. Sometimes it is hard to dream.

Taking a survival job may be necessary.

After the dot-com crash there was not much work for recruiters. I started a new company making house calls to repair computers. It was not really what I wanted to be doing. I was good at it, and it helped to pay the bills.

Call me a dreamer, but I think that it is possible for every person to be working at a job they enjoy.

Imagine a world where every person was happy with the work they were doing. Imagine how much happier a place the world would be. Like I said, I dream big.

Do not give up. I think you can find what you are looking for. But you still have to eat on your way there.

CHAPTER THREE: For the Employed

Why are you looking?
If you are employed and want to look for a new position, ask yourself why.

Look at the things you have or do not have in your current position.

Look at what you want.

How much of a difference is there?

Is a job search worth the time and energy and stress?

Changing jobs is on the list of the 10 most stressful things in life.

I am not saying that you should not change your job, but I advise looking at alternatives first. Sometimes it is easier to change things about your current employment than it is to find a new position.

When I interview people, I often ask them why they are looking for a new position. Sometimes after a discussion, candidates find that they do not really want to change jobs. Frequently, they can change aspects of their jobs. Sometimes you can get moved away from the person who hiccups all day long. Or you can get a new phone or maybe an upgraded computer. Or a better budget for your projects.

My point here is that you should first identify why you want to change jobs, and then determine whether any of those things can be fixed. The effort to change some aspects of a job you are already working at can be a lot less work than finding a new position. You need to look at the job objectively and you need to have the desire to make some changes.

This assumes that you are mostly happy with your job.

If you hate your job, boss, or company, then it will probably be best for everyone that you find something new.

I have seen plenty of people who move to a new job and are not happy that they did. Think before you jump.

If you are just looking for a raise

Often, for a variety of reasons, people need to be earning more money. Maybe the person is a star performer and wants appropriate pay. Maybe there are huge medical bills at home. Needing better compensation is a valid reason for considering a new job.

Getting a job offer from another company may not be the best way if you are looking to get more money in your current position.

If you like your work, company and team, do not go looking for a job so you can use a job offer to force your employer to give you a significant raise.

It may not work the way you want it to.

If you go to your boss, tell them you have a job offer with a different company, but that you'd prefer to stay because you just want a raise, odds are good that you will get the money if it is available. But you may also have earned the distrust of your boss, who will always be worried that you are looking to move on. You could miss out on internal opportunities because your boss will look to your coworkers who have not used a job offer to force a raise.

Your best bet starts with market research. Compare your pay rate to the market rates for similar workers at comparable-size companies in your region.

If you discover that you are underpaid, take your findings to your boss and ask for a raise.

Realize that you need to do more than ask for a raise. You need to be prepared to show why you deserve it. Just showing that your pay is below market rates will not be enough. You need to show the value that you provide to the company. Look at your accomplishments and be prepared to make a case for your raise.

While I think that asking for a raise is better and easier than a job search, do not expect the process to be easy. In some companies there are piles of paperwork and processes to follow. Most of the work will need to be done by your direct manager, so your case for a raise needs to be solid. You may need to be patient.

If you do not get the raise, and if getting more money is important, then you can start looking for a new position with better pay.

Improving compensation

In many industries, and many positions, the best way to improve your pay is a job change.

Unfortunate but true.

Well, maybe not unfortunate for me. If most companies gave better raises, then people would not change jobs so often, and I would have a whole lot less work to do.

Here is how it works.

The average yearly raise is about 3%[1]. You could get less than that if your company is not doing well, or if you have not performed to company standards. A strong performer might get 4 percent.

However, the cost of living goes up by about 2 percent a year[2].

The result is that people who stay in a job get about a 1% increase every year. This does not properly address increasing experience and seniority.

A new job can often provide a compensation increase of 5 percent to 20 percent (your mileage may vary according to industry, geographic area, and position). If you change jobs every two years, then this adds up quickly. Over a lifetime, a person who changes jobs every two years can make 50 percent more lifetime income than a person who stays in one job.

Yes, there are potential problems with changing jobs so frequently (I have more to say on this in the next topic).

The bottom line is that unless you are in one of those rare companies that gives high salary increases, changing jobs is the road to better compensation.

Be careful. If possible, work to a plan. Change positions in a time frame that works for you, but also is reasonable in the industry you are in.

---

[1] www.bls.gov/news.release/eci.nr0.htm
[2] www.data.bls.gov/timeseries/CUUR0000SA0?output_view=pct_12mth

Frequency of job change

Question from a candidate: Do frequent job changes look bad on your résumé? Do people care about this?

The length of time people stay in jobs is dependent on the industry, but also on the number of people in that industry who do contract or temporary work. Since contract work is most often of shorter duration than being directly employed, this can make the average employment time look shorter.

You need to look up the average duration of employment in your own industry and compare your employment periods to that. Note that the general trend has been toward shorter employment periods. The days when people would work for one company until they retired are almost gone.

Companies are smaller and leaner and tend to hire and lay off people more quickly than they had been doing 20 or more years ago. This also contributes to people's having more frequent job changes

To directly answer the question, usually it does not look bad anymore. Some people will always think the opposite, that having more than one or two jobs on your résumé means that you are disloyal and won't even interview you. This is getting less common, however.

You would be better off trying to keep your average employment duration longer than the average for your industry.

Companies that care the most about long tenure are those that have positions that require a long time to be proficient, like a geospatial algorithm engineer. A company would probably not hire someone into this position who has been changing jobs every two to three years, unless there was a good reason.

Reduced working hours

Question from a candidate: Is it possible to work part time in order to devote more time to something else?

This depends on the industry and the position. Some jobs are hard to do with less than an average of 40 hours per week, i.e., many research and technical positions.

I do not know of many professional positions that are part-time.

Some companies are starting job-share programs, where they hire two part-time people who share a job. Between the two people, they work 40 hours per week. This seems to be an increasing but slow-moving trend.

Some universities have shorter work weeks than industry positions. I was once employed by a university where I worked a 35-hour week, and had great benefits, including a good amount of vacation time. The pay was not great, but the job was worth it, given the other benefits.

Some companies reduce the number of hours their people work so the company can avoid providing benefits. While it may allow for personal flexibility, keeping employee hours low to dodge benefits is not something that would fire my interest in an employer.

How do you find a job like this?

Ask your current employer if a reduction in hours would be possible. I know several people that have successfully done this, including some who wanted more time to be with their children. Changing the job you are in is likely easier than finding a new part-time position.

One key to finding a position like this is to focus on your efficiency. Show how you can be very effective in short time periods.

Moving up

Question from a candidate: I want to lead a team; should I change jobs or stay where I am?

I think you should start where you are. Are you happy with your current company, peers, managers and work? If so, then it would be best to start from your current position. Have a private meeting with your manager about your goals. Ask about a shift in responsibilities.

What do your managers think about your doing this? Do they think you are qualified? Need training? Have the right or wrong personality? Hope that you have a good manager who will give you honest feedback.

In addition, talk to peers (at lunch or outside of work would be best), friends or previous managers. Ask the same questions.

To be blunt, the point here is to gather multiple opinions about what others think about your ability to lead a team. If you get a lot of negative feedback, it does not mean that you cannot do it, but that you might need some training or education. Or you might need a job coach. This is especially important before you go looking for a new external job that includes leading. You do not want to mess up a job you currently enjoy for one that you might not even like.

If you have received good feedback, and if your boss is supportive, work with your boss to find a project where you can take the lead. The best thing about this is that you can try it out without leaving behind the safety of a job you like.

When you have finished with the project, take an honest look at it. Did you like it? Was it successful? Did you learn about leading? Talk with your boss about the same things to get feedback. Do you want to keep doing it? If not, you can stay in your regular job. If it worked, you could work with your boss (or others in the company as needed) to continue to work in that direction.

Overall, this is a safe way to transition (or not) into leadership.

It gets more difficult when there is no opportunity for leadership in your current position. It might be because nothing is available, or maybe your boss is not willing to support you. Then you can consider looking for positions outside of the company.

The problem is that you do not know whether you like leading, or whether you are good at it. It will also be tough to interview for, and land, a job where you do not have the experience the employer is looking for.

My suggestion would be to get some leadership experience outside of work first. Coach a kids' sports team or lead a volunteer activity. Try something that involves leadership to see whether you are good at it and like it.

Assess your skills. Get feedback from others. Work into it gradually. The worst-case scenario here would be to move to a new job leading a team, only to find that you are not good at it or do not like it. Then you would need to find a way to transition back to the work you like.

CHAPTER FOUR: Self-Assessment

You were not trained for this

I got fired from the-company-that-shall-not-be-named and went home and started working. The funny thing is that I was essentially doing the same things that I had been doing at the office. I was looking for companies with open positions. I had training for this. This is not normal.

When you are unemployed your "job" is to find a new job. You did not go to school for this. There are no degrees for this. If you went to college, your school career center might have helped with a seminar on writing résumés and maybe one about interviewing.

If you have been laid off by a big corporation, you might have been sent to an outplacement service that would help you find a new job. (And as a side note, it is often worth it for the company to do this ... even a tenth of a point on its unemployment insurance rate can mean huge amounts of money it is paying on remaining employees. It is in the company's best interest for you to find employment quickly and stop collecting unemployment checks.)

My point is that you were not trained to do this full time. Do not have expectations that you will be an expert.

For that matter, do not expect that you will find a job quickly. It might go quickly; it might be exceedingly slow. It depends on your location, industry, unemployment rates, etc.

What can you do?

Be open. Listen. Learn. Take classes and go to seminars. Look for help. Ask for help. Accept help where it is offered. Your job search will go much easier — and possibly faster — if you think of yourself as a beginner and try to be a knowledge sponge.

The mind resists change

When you do anything in your life, and do it many times, your brain sets down neural pathways. The more you do something, the more your brain gets entrenched in that activity.

This is not a flaw. This is brain specialization.

Our brains are amazing at getting good at something. When it is something important, when it is a survival skill (which your job is) your brain makes it easier for you to do that job. The tasks you do regularly get easier.

The problem comes when something shakes up your life.

A job search is like that. By the nature of it you disrupt the primary daily paths your brain uses. This is hard. The brain is resistant to change. You may have spent many years specializing and building those neural pathways. Changing them is tough.

Sometimes it even makes you sick. It is very common for people to get sick after they have lost a job. Stress, depression or anxiety may be factors as well. Your brain needs time to adjust. It needs down time.

It goes back to balance. You need to give yourself time to rest, play, grieve. Give yourself time to adjust.

Once you start to build those new neural pathways in the brain your job search will get easier.

The ideal job

The ideal job. The perfect job. The dream job.

Possible or unrealistic?

Think about what you want in a job.

Would you like a job that has broad or narrow responsibilities? Do you like a job that is the same every day or that changes every day?

Is it important that you love or like what you do?

Do you like a large or a small company? Or a startup?

Do you enjoy working with people? With large or small groups? Do you prefer to work alone?

Do you like to be your own boss? Are you independent or a team player or both?

What kind of work environment do you like? Do you like flexible hours? Fixed hours?

Open environment or private space?

Your job search is not just about the skills you use every day. It is about finding a position that fits you. And that fit is much broader than your specific skill set.

Take some time to look at what you want outside of your skill set. Make a list if that works for you. Be aware of your own preferences.

Your perfect job is about more than your skill set, and you are more likely to find it if you are aware of what you like.

Think about these for now. Later you will use these to make your career marketing plan.

Know yourself

I am an introvert. I enjoy getting to know people but not introducing myself. I think about decisions exhaustively, then make them emotionally. I like to have a regular schedule. But I do not like to plan. I am creative, innovative and tenacious. But that same tenacity sometimes gets me stuck and makes me inflexible.

One of my clients does a personality test before hiring managers. The client let me take the test. It was not a big surprise that it told me I like to do things my own way and would be better self-employed than working for someone else. It was accurate.

Who are you? What are your strengths?

To go into a job search you should have a strong awareness of yourself, your strengths and weaknesses.

There are books and online tests to help you get to know yourself better.

Your friends will always be willing to give you their opinions. A career coach can help.

Maybe you know yourself well. Maybe you do not. Some people are naturally more introspective. Some people do not think it is all that important.

Whatever your natural inclination, it is important to know yourself before you get into interviews. Most people who interview you will have their own special questions meant to throw you off guard.

Knowing yourself is one key to being able to answer those questions well.

Shaman's death

Once upon a time I was troubled over a change that was happening in my life. I was wandering through a New Age bookstore and came across a box of cards, similar to tarot cards except with a Native American perspective, called Sacred Path Cards. I was interested so I picked them up and looked at a card.

Shaman's Death. I read the description. I do not remember the exact wording, but it was something like "to make room for something new to grow you may need to let something die. To do something new you may need to let go of something old."

I was stunned. I had been wanting to do something new, but I kept falling back into the old. I needed to let go of the old (and maybe grieve) to have room for the new to grow.

You can look at it like the closets in your house or apartment. When they get full, it is time to get rid of some old things, especially if you want to put something new there. (Let's ignore the trend to rent storage space for stuff that people do not use and do not want to throw away.)

Your mind and heart are the same way. You need to let go of the old job and the old way of doing things to make room for the new job. Especially if you want things that are different.

I am not saying this is easy. The word "death" on that card was not an accident. Letting go can be hard, hard enough that there are people who write entire books about it.

Why are you on this planet?

I have another question that I consider to be spiritual. I like to help people find better work. I think that if people find work they like, they will be happier. More happy people make the world a better place. I help to make the world better by helping people find jobs they enjoy.

What is the next thing you want to accomplish with your life? Why are you here?

I believe that everyone on this planet has a purpose. Some may know what it is and some may not.

If you do not know your purpose, I believe that it is worth discovering.

Some may have accomplished their first purpose. Sometimes these people move on to the next thing. Some people wander for a while trying to figure out what the next thing is. It is OK to have more than one purpose in life.

Purpose provides drive and motivation. It helps you to get up every day and to get things done.

Some people go to work every day to bring home a paycheck to provide for their family. Some people cannot go to work unless they know their work is doing something helpful for someone else.

Why are you here? What is next for you? What difference do you want to make in the world?

I can provide only the questions for this one. You need to provide the answers.

What is your passion?

If you look back at all the jobs you have held, all the things you have done, what common threads can you find in all of those? What parts of a job or task did you enjoy regardless of the circumstances?

Writer/mystic Sam Keen calls this the Peanut Butter Principle. Through all the things he has done throughout his life, all the jobs he has held, he has always loved peanut butter. Whatever he does next he will always love peanut butter.

What do you love? What are the things you think about in your past that bring you joy? What aspects are common to all the things you have done that you have loved?

Look for that in your next job. Look for those threads of joy that have been common throughout your entire life.

If you do not find that in your next job, you might not be there very long.

If you find it, you will do your job better, with more passion. You will make a difference and be happier.

What if you cannot figure out what your passion is? What if there is no common thread?

Search. Play. Experiment.

There are plenty of books about this, about finding your strengths and passions. Some of them might be fun for you. Go to a library or bookstore and get a few.

Take courses that interest you. Many high schools have adult education courses that are very inexpensive and not very time-intensive.

Read a book about a career you think you might like. If you cannot finish the book then, you know one more thing you do not want to do.

Some people know their passion. Some people have to look for it under every rock. Some people get hit over the head with the idea, like writing a book for job seekers.

What is great about you?

This is a question that I often ask people, typically when working on a résumé that seems to lack direction.

What is great about you?

I have been accused of being an optimist many times, but despite that I still believe the following is true: Everyone has something that is great about them.

I am very good about getting to know a subject in depth. Like recruiting. Once I get to know the subject, I can be innovative and creative and find new and better ways to do things.

You may not know what your greatest attribute is. Your friends should know. Your coworkers would know. Ask people.

You may know. Or it may be something that you have not developed yet.

This is your biggest selling point. You need to know what this is.

This needs to be on your résumé.

You need to bring it up in interviews. I am not saying to flaunt it or be conceited. Be confident in your strength.

What is great about you?

Changing careers

Changing careers. To clarify this topic is changing what you do for work, not just whom you work for.

It is wonderful when your current employer offers you responsibilities in a new direction that you want to explore, and a new career is started. But that does not happen all that often.

Do you want to change careers? Why? Here are some of the most common reasons (not in order):

- Tired. Burnt out. Exhausted. Stressed. At wit's end.
- Laid off. You do not like the job.
- New passion.
- No jobs.
- Better money.
- Better opportunities or advancement.

I started as a software engineer. I did not plan to become a network administrator, but I found the job after I had been laid off, and I had enough transferable skills to make it work. I did not plan to become a recruiter, but when I was asked to interview for the position, my previous technical background helped it work out. That is two career changes, one minor and one major.

I am now working on the next one. I would like to become a full-time writer. This one is taking more work. It means using some of my free time to learn to write better, to practice, and to work on my books. It is not easy or fast, but I am working on it and keeping my day job while I do that.

If you are working, I would suggest against quitting your current job to dive into the new profession. Talk with a career counselor or coach first. Look objectively at the new career to determine whether it will really work. Come up with a plan. Take your time if that is an option.

Maybe you do not need a new career. Maybe you just need to do some volunteer work to rebuild your energy. Or find a new hobby you are passionate about.

If you are going to make a career change, you will need a new résumé that focuses on transferable skills, that shows relevant experience and projects. You might also need help with this, because it will be selling yourself differently than you did before.

Changing careers is tough. Realizing that makes it easier for you to handle the challenges — one after another — that you encounter as you try to navigate your transition.

Persistence

Nothing can replace persistence.

When I was first starting as a recruiter I talked with a candidate who later found himself a job with a startup company. Every month I called him to ask him how things were going and if he needed recruiting help. We talked about the company's growth and direction. Sometimes I just left him a voicemail. Sometimes we had long conversations.

For six years I called him every month.

Then one day he had some work for me. He had a position he needed help filling.

I have been working with that company for about 12 years now. I fill about one position a year for them as they grow.

Persistence. Tenacity. Call it what you will. You need to keep trying.

You also need balance. If I had called that same person every week, he probably would have stopped taking my calls in the first year because I was being annoying.

Ask people for permission to call people back or to send an email. Ask what the right time period would be. Put that in your notebook or contact manager.

Persistence, with balance, works.

I know one candidate, Tom, who calls me every week when he is out of work. Unfortunately, he has worked for a few companies that did not do well and has been through several layoffs. He has taken contract jobs so he could continue to pay his bills. He does not give up. I can rely on his call every week when he is looking for new work.

If I worked with you as a candidate, could I rely on your checking in with me every week?

Career coach

An option to consider is a career coach. If you are employed (so cannot use state or federal sponsored programs) a career coach is an excellent option. Even if you are unemployed and use those services, you can still hire a career coach.

Depending on their expertise they can provide coaching on résumé creation, interviewing, networking, career path, education options, personality tests, and more.

This is not the same as a staffing agency or headhunter. Coaches rarely work with companies to place you, though they are typically well-connected and can put you in touch with other people who might also help your career. Sometimes this can include contacts at your target companies.

Rates vary but are generally hourly.

If you are unemployed, these costs can be written off on your taxes as part of a job search.

Here are two that I recommend. If you are in the Rochester, New York, area, you can see them in person; otherwise both will do coaching remotely as well.
- Kathleen Pringle: www.kathleenpringle.com
- Hannah Morgan: www.careersherpa.net

CHAPTER FIVE: Prepare

General
Some general preparation items to help make your job search easier and more efficient:
- If possible, set aside a space that is specifically for your job search, especially if you are not employed and will work there regularly.
- Make sure you have a professional sounding email address. Some people create a second email address that they use specifically for job search activities. That helps them ensure nothing is overlooked.
- Make sure your voicemail message and/or answering message sound professional.
- Review your wardrobe for proper clothes for the job you want. If it is lacking, start making improvements right away. You do not want to discover at the last minute that your best shirt has a coffee stain on it.

Set goals
Goal setting blah blah blah.

How many times have you heard this in your life? Have you done it? Almost every person I have ever asked has been taught methods of goal setting. Few put those methods into practice.

As someone who does not particularly like to plan, I am not very consistent. But I can tell you that if I make a list of goals for the day, I will always accomplish more than on a day when I do not set goals.

A set of goals is more than a task list. I make long task lists just so I can remember everything that needs to be done. Make a task list if that helps you, but also make a list of goals for the day, week, month.

I like the concepts in SMART goals.

Specific: do not generalize.

Measurable: you should be able to tell whether it is completed or not.

Achievable: Setting smaller goals that can be reached is better.

Realistic: Do not set goals dependent on other people, or the weather.

Timely: today, this week, this month. The point is to get it done, not put it off.

I will not delve into more detail on this one. If you are interested, there are dozens of websites complete with worksheets that you can use to set good goals. There are phone apps to give you reminders.

I know one person who does a lot of contract work. When he is out of work, he calls me every week. He has a schedule and a list of tasks. It works to help him find his next contract.

Even if you do not use goal setting in the rest of your life, I recommend it for the time you are in job search mode. It will help you find a new job more efficiently.

Track job search activity

Make a list. Make lots of lists.

One thing that annoys me is when a candidate does not keep track of her or his job search.

For example, I do a phone interview with a candidate. After the interview portion, I tell the candidate about possible jobs. When there is interest in particular jobs, I provide more detail about the client, including the company name, culture and history. After further discussion, if the candidate is interested in the job, I ask permission to send the résumé. If that is approved, I send over the résumé, with an interview sheet, to my client.

The frustrating part comes when the client sends back a message saying that they had already received the résumé of the candidate. I then contact the candidate to ask about that previous application. The response is almost always that the candidate had forgotten that it had previously been done.

It does not say much about a candidate that cannot remember where their résumé has been sent. When clients receive a résumé from more than one source, whether it is from two recruiters or from one recruiter and one direct from the candidate, the most common response from the company is to remove the candidate from the list of candidates being considered.

The solution is simple: Track your job search activity.

Record every email, résumé submission, phone call, lunch meeting, conversation with a recruiter (and their résumé submissions on your behalf). It will avoid duplication problems. It will help you follow up with companies and recruiters. It might even make you look good when you can cite dates and times your résumé was submitted.

In some states they require this logging if you want to collect unemployment checks.

One a related note, some jobs require people to log other activity, like sales and technical support positions. Why not just continue this at home for the job search? It is worth your time and effort.

Elevator pitch

I am sure that you have heard this dozens of times, maybe hundreds, that you need to have a good elevator pitch. I have read dozens of descriptions, and they can include:
- Be brief (depending on the perspective, typically 30 or 60 seconds).
- Be clear.
- Say who you are, what you do and why you do it.
- Say who you do it for and how they benefit.
- Show the problems you solve and your approach.
- Give your USP (unique selling proposition).
- Have a follow-up question to engage the person you are speaking with.
- Practice.

The one that I almost never hear:
- Be authentic.

The reason many people have trouble giving an elevator pitch, and why many people sound fake, is that they are not being authentic. I have found that it helps to think of the pitch as a conversation, not a formal presentation. Think about how you would normally answer the questions above during a normal conversation with a friend. Write that down and practice that. It will come across as more authentic and conversational, rather than forced as a contrived speech into someone's eardrums.

Business cards?

Do you need to have job search business cards?

Need? No. Will they help? Maybe. Will they hurt? No.

It is worth having some while you are looking for a new position.

They do not cost much. If you are unemployed, you can often find a printing company that will make some for you free. I get some nice Avery Clean Edge cards and print my own. You probably do not need a lot.

What should they have on them?
- Title or very short sales pitch
- Your name
- Your contact information

You can add other things if you like but remember that the card is not the sales pitch. You are the sales pitch. The card is just the reminder for the contact, so they can reach you if needed.

When do you give them?
- Job fairs
- Networking events
- Interviews
- At your kid's baseball game, the grocery store, or anywhere you might meet people who can help in your job search.

Some people I know always have their own card, because they are always networking and looking for the next big project or job.

Know your market value

To begin, it is best to know your own numbers. Look at your monthly budget (you have a monthly budget, right?) so you know how much you need to make to get by. The bottom line is that you need to know your own bottom line. Then you need a target number roughly 10 percent above that. Now you have your starting range. These are not numbers that you are going to give to a company or a recruiter; they are for you.

The next step is to gather market data. This one is simple in theory but tougher in practice. You will need to gather your data from many sources.

Depending on the size of your employer, you can start with HR. Ask for the pay range of your current position. If you are worried about their thinking that you might be looking for a new employer, then ask for the range of the next higher position. Ask about what it takes to get a promotion. That should get you information about salary ranges from your current employer's perspective. And it will give the impression that you want to move to a better position, which might be what you want.

An alternative would be to find other people you know in HR, possibly in places you worked before. They may not be allowed to give you that information because you do not work for them, but it is worth a try.

Next, use your network. Confidentially ask other people you know how much they are making and how many years of experience they have. If they do not want to reveal their salary you can always ask the reverse. "How much should a person in my position, with five years of experience, be making?" Talking about salaries is still taboo in some places so you can expect some resistance. I have been a recruiter for so long that I am immune to this. I talk about salary very casually, as if it is normal, which it is for me, and I get very little resistance.

Be cautious asking current co-workers about their salary. Some companies have policies that prohibit this, and in some cases it is grounds for termination. Check your employee manual first. In addition, salary discussions can cause internal conflicts when some people find out that others are making more than they are.

Use salary websites. My present favorite is www.payscale.com. It takes a little more time to enter all your information into the system but when you do, it presents detailed information about the salary range for your position, including size of company and location. It provides a much more detailed salary report, including a bell curve of related salaries. In my experience, most salary sites have numbers that are 10 to 20 percent higher than actual market numbers, so be cautious about how you use the numbers.

Look up any local salary surveys. Sometimes you can find one made by the local Chamber of Commerce.

Another source you can use is a recruiter. If you have a good relationship with a local recruiter, you can ask the same question and get a good range for your market value. If you are contacting a new recruiter, make sure that the person has expertise in your career area. I will happily have a conversation with a possible new candidate about local salaries for the types of positions I fill.

Your last step is to compare your personal needs to your present position salary and then to the results from your research. This should provide you with an accurate market value.

About references

Before you start your search, you need to start a list of professional references. They do not need to be complete before you start looking but should be finished before you start interviews. These should be kept in a separate file from your résumé, to be provided when requested. Sometimes you will need your references for an online application and most of the time when filling out a written application.

Some companies will call your references before they bring you in for an interview but more often they will be called after you interview, if the company is considering making you an offer. Since you do not know when references are going to be called, it is best to have your list completed early.

It may be that references will not be needed in the future. There is considerable discussion now about whether they provide any value. After all, you are providing the prospective employer the names of people you know will say good things about you. When I do reference checks, I do them differently from most companies. I like to ask questions to better understand how the candidate works, and what things will help that person be successful. A few other companies are doing this, but it does not seem to be a trend.

Many companies have policies against their people providing references to previous employees. They are generally worried about lawsuits. You can expect resistance from some people because of company policy, but if the reference likes you, they will most often ignore the policy and help you.

Getting references

I was calling references for Jane, who was getting a job offer from one of my clients. It turned out that one reference, Dick, did not actually like Jane, because she received the promotion that he wanted. He said quite unpleasant things about her. The good news is that two other references had stellar things to say about Jane, and the client offered her the job and she accepted. Dick's attempt to sabotage her new job failed.

The lesson for you is to do your best to make sure that your reference will say good things about you. If someone really dislikes you, they might lie anyway, but better to at least try to know. This example does not occur often, but it pays to be careful.

To start, ask permission to use someone as a reference. I think that you should ask it in a very particular way. "Would you be willing to be a favorable reference for me?" The word "favorable" is important.

If you get resistance or waffling, let the person know that it is OK, and let them off. If the person is reacting in that way, they might not have great things to say about you. Move on to the next person.

Your references should be people whom you have worked with and can offer favorably objective details of your work. Typically I ask for four references from people; two managers and two co-workers. The managers should be direct supervisors; people who have a strong knowledge of you. Co-workers' references can also be friends; just make sure they talk about you as a co-worker and leave out anything outside of work.

I suggest that you provide the mobile number for your references. References tend to be very busy people and are much easier to reach with a mobile number. This can also help if the references have to dodge company policy.

I also prefer that you provide the current employer of your reference and the reference's current title. This allows the recruiter to call the reference and not have to ask them too many questions about themselves. Sometimes asking questions like that can get people defensive because they think they are being recruited, which makes it harder to complete the reference check.

Do not provide references until they are needed. Some agencies try to recruit your references, which will annoy your references. Be courteous of their time.

CHAPTER SIX: Career Marketing Plan

What is a career marketing plan?

In 2012 I received my first career marketing plan from a candidate. I was interested and intrigued. I wanted to work with her and help her find her next position. A week later she had found a new position and was no longer on the market.

This has been true of almost every candidate that sent me a career marketing plan. It seemed to me that the candidates would just disappear off the market. A candidate with a plan would find a new position much quicker than most candidates.

It is effective. It works. It is the best thing that you can do to accelerate your job search.

What is it?

A marketing plan is not a résumé, though the format may look like one.

It is a document to detail the goals of your job search and help you achieve those goals. It helps to make your job search more efficient, effective and focused.

In previous topics I suggested you think about your goals and passions. I asked you to think about what you want. Now is the time to put those things down in writing.

There is no prescribed format for these. Some sections are common to most of the plans I have seen and some are seldom used. Use whichever elements are relevant to your own search.

Make it look nice, just as you want your résumé to look professionally presented.

What do you do with it?

- Use it to focus your job search on a daily and weekly basis, to generate tasks to complete.
- Give it to people you are talking with. It is a great tool to open conversations. Every time someone reads it they will have questions and suggestions for you. It is much more effective than a résumé for getting help and tips.
- Do not send it in along with your résumé when applying for a job.

Elements or sections

Here are the elements I have most often seen in an effective career marketing plan:

- Pitch/positioning statement/branding statement/objective: Similar to an elevator pitch, it should be short and concise. It should reflect your passion and priorities.
- Skills/work functions/competencies: What work do you want to be doing? What are you best at? What are your primary skills?
- Value/value-add/strengths/differentiation: What makes you different from everyone else on the market? What is great about you?
- Target geography. If not in the area you currently work, what locations are you open to?
- Target industries: If applicable, what industries would you prefer to work in?
- Target companies: A list of companies that you would consider working for. Typically, this list is at least 20 companies. This item is the best conversation generator. People will tell you about the companies they like and dislike, and why. They may suggest other companies for your list. If they do not initiate suggestions, it's a great idea to ask for some.

Here are some elements I see occasionally:

- Market assessment: What is the market like for your profession? Are job openings common or scarce? Are salaries rising or falling? What is the unemployment rate?
- Achievement: A short list of your favorite achievements.
- Target culture: What aspects of culture would you like to see in your next employer?
- Target size: Do you have a preference for the company size of your next employer? And why?
- Time frame: What is your time frame for starting a new position?
- Plan: What specific steps you are taking to get your next position (see also topic on goal setting).

CHAPTER SIX: Career Marketing Plan

- Audience: What people are your target audience for this document?
- Compensation: What salary, pay rate and benefits are you looking for?
- Promotional methods: What promotional methods are you using? What networks are you working with?

General thoughts:
- Have a title like "Career Marketing Plan" centered at the top so people do not think the document is your résumé.
- Try to keep the document easily readable, plenty of white space, reasonable type size and confined to a single page.

CHAPTER SEVEN: Cover Letters

Do you need a cover letter?

Maybe. Unfortunately, like some other topics there is no single answer for this one either.

I can tell you that most recruiters do not read cover letters. Most will go straight to the résumé. I know some recruiters who read cover letters. It is not common but there are some.

Will you get rejected if you do not write a cover letter? I have never heard of this happening.

Does it hurt to write a cover letter? No. It might help. If it gets read, it can point out things that cannot often be easily shown in a résumé.

If you write a cover letter, it should include something different from what is in your résumé. It should not just restate what is already in the other document.

There are also some Applicant Tracking Systems (ATS) that allow you to enter a cover letter. These are attached to your record in the ATS, so if the ATS suggests one then it is probably worth doing, because if someone is looking you up in an ATS, they may see the cover letter.

Do not put a cover letter in the same document as your résumé. It will often annoy recruiters, especially those in agencies. This is because they will have to edit your résumé to remove the cover letter (though they will sometimes save the cover letter as a separate file, but that is also more work) if they want to send it to a client. You may also need it as a separate document to upload to an ATS.

I suggest writing a cover letter. It may not get read, but there is a chance that it will get read, and if someone reads it, it should improve your chances at getting an interview.

If you are going to write a cover letter, do it right. The primary reason that recruiters do not read cover letters is because most are too long, too wordy and unclear.

What is in a good cover letter?

A good cover letter is short and concise. Equally important, it sells.

It consists of three paragraphs. Each paragraph should have about two sentences. Uppermost, it should be a quick and easy read.

Do not repeat what is in the résumé.

What might each paragraph say?

- How did you hear about the job?
- What contacts do you have at the company?
- Why are you interested in the position or company?
- Something that makes you uniquely qualified.
- Describe how you can excel at the tasks they need completed.
- Express appreciation and that you hope to hear from them soon, and a date at which you will follow up.

Or include other things that you think might trigger the reader's interest that may be specific to your profession. But at most three brief paragraphs.

If you make it too long, it will not get read. It will get opened, but the recruiter, upon seeing how long it is, will close it without reading anything and proceed to your résumé.

How important is tailoring the cover letter?

Very. I cannot tell you how many times I have received cover letters that were addressed to someone else. Please modify all details related to the company you are contacting.

It is important that you address the cover letter to a specific person, ideally the hiring manager, or possibly the HR representative.

Double-check spelling and grammar, just as you would on a résumé.

Alternate cover letter

An alternate type of cover letter can work.

It includes a T chart. This is a table with two columns.

On one side it lists the qualifications detailed in the job description. The other side shows how you meet those qualifications.

These are most effective when it may not be clear from your résumé that you are qualified for the position. Again, you are not duplicating what is in the résumé, but adding clarification.

I know some people who say that such T chart cover letters are very effective.

As a recruiter I cannot say that I have received many of these, or that they have been especially effective. But then I do not often open cover letters.

I am not a normal recruiter in some ways. If the résumé is reasonably well-written, I can often sift things out of it to determine whether someone is qualified, even if it may not be initially apparent. If I think that the person may be qualified, I will send an email to get clarification or schedule a quick call. I can do this without looking at the cover letter.

The T chart may work for you. It is a good alternative if you are not a normal applicant for a position, or if your qualifications may not be easily apparent from your résumé, possibly because of a potential career change.

CHAPTER EIGHT: All About Résumés

Overview

I have some different perspectives here. I have read a lot of résumés. I have done some research on how people read, and talked with a lot of other recruiters about how they read résumés.

This section is filled with hints on how to make your résumé effective. An effective résumé will get you an interview. That is it. The résumé has only one purpose. If it does not get you an interview, for a job for which you are qualified, then it has failed and needs adjustment.

A résumé is a sales document. It does not need to be as complicated as many people make it. It needs to be as simple as possible to get the point across. It does not need to have all the details. Depending on your format or age, it may not even have all your work history.

Think about an advertisement you see for any product you remember and that gets you to buy the product. Does it have a lot of text? Is the ad complicated? Does it work?

Does your résumé do that? Does it work to get you interviews? Do readers "buy" and bring you in for an interview? If it does not get you in the door, you need to fix it. You need to make it more effective. Usually this means making it shorter and more effective.

Make your résumé simple and direct. If you provide the recruiter or hiring manager with the information they are looking for, in a way that is quick and easy to read, you will get an interview. That is all there is to it. If you do not have a résumé, you can find a template online. Or you can start from scratch using the information in the following résumé-related topics.

Or you can get help. If you went to college, or are finishing college now, I suggest investigating the career center at your school. It is very likely that they have people who can help you with your résumé. Colleges are getting more competitive, and one item that helps them to get new students is their placement percentage. To do a good job placing graduates, they need to teach them how to write résumés.

Summary: The résumé is a sales document whose purpose is to get you an interview. Nothing more.

Contrarian views

I have already told you I am not a normal recruiter.

Like many recruiters I have looked at countless résumés. I have paid attention to how I read a résumé. I have asked other recruiters how they read résumés.

I have paid attention to what works when I send résumés to my clients.

I know what things make my life easier as a recruiter.

Some of my ideas on résumés are contrary to popular opinion. Some are often just not discussed. Some fall in line with what other recruiters think.

My opinion on a résumé's having an objective is one contrarian example. I think most résumés should have one. Many other recruiters disagree.

Try these ideas out. See what works for you. My methods will not work for everyone in every profession. To get more relevant ideas about this, I recommend finding a recruiter who works specifically with your profession.

One problem with résumés is that people expect a somewhat normal format. That makes it tough to stand out. If you carefully craft a résumé, with a mix of standard and nonstandard methods, in an easy to read format, you should be able to sell yourself well.

How recruiters read résumés

First, recruiters do not read your résumé. They skim your résumé. Some recruiters are exceptions (and they get mad at me if I do not include this exception).

Recruiters usually will know roughly what they are looking for.

First, they know the title of the open position. They will scan the top of your résumé for something that looks equivalent.

They have a list of required skill sets. They will scan your résumé for some of those, whether you put them in a table (easy) or line of text (hard).

They know the company culture and will scan for items that show them a match.

They will scan through your work experience for titles that look similar to what they are looking for. They will scan for long-term employment and interesting company names and job titles.

That is about it. You have somewhere between five and 10 seconds to provide that information for them.

If they see some of what they are looking for, you will have earned more time. The recruiter will look in more detail at skill sets and job experience to make sure they are a fit before sending the résumé to the actual hiring manager. Agencies are a little different from internal recruiters, and I will discuss this more in a later topic.

If the recruiter will be doing a phone interview with you, they will generally read more of the résumé, but only if you pass the initial inspection.

The hiring manager will generally read most of the résumé. They will read the first page, skim other pages and read things that look interesting to them. Some hiring managers will read the entire résumé. Much of what determines whether the manager will read the résumé is the style of the manager and the related industry for the open position.

You do not have much time to make a good impression. Use it well.

Slogging through résumés

One day while I was working, a candidate called me to check in. During our discussion, I told him I "was slogging through résumés." He was offended. He believed that looking at résumés was an important part of my job and that I should not be applying such a derogatory term to that. He even suggested that if I did not like looking at résumés that much, it should not be my job.

News flash: Looking at résumés usually is not fun. It is hard work and often very annoying. The biggest reason for this is that most résumés are written poorly. It is not much fun to look at a résumé and have the task of trying to figure out what the person does and wants.

Occasionally I would come across a very nicely made résumé, or one that was very creative, and those were enjoyable to look at. Those are not common.

Big hint: If you make it easy and fun for the recruiter, your chances of getting an interview are much higher!

When I tried to explain this to the candidate, he did not agree. He did not think that he should have to modify his résumé to make it easier for the recruiter. He clearly did not understand the purpose of a résumé.

Visual perspective

The visual perspective of a résumé:
- Getting an understanding of how the résumé looks as a whole, and the first impression the reader takes away before he even reads a single word.
- Placing information in the résumé in a format such that the reader quickly and easily sees the information you want the person to see.

Take a printed résumé and hold it at arm's length.

How does it look? Packed? Empty? Are the sections crowded together or spaced well?

Move the résumé closer and give yourself 10 seconds to look at it. What stands out? Typically, the items that will stand out are any items that are along the left side, in a larger font, or that are bold. Are those the things you want to stand out?

Are there too many items in bold or italics? It is noisy? What do you see first?

Move the résumé to normal reading distance. As you scan down the page, what else do you notice? Primary skills? Titles? Employers?

Are the things you are drawn to on the résumé the things that you want the reader to see?

What you have done is to review the effectiveness of the formatting of your résumé. You have looked to see if it is visually effective. And this without really looking at most of the data in the résumé.

Three green lights

Another way to look at how recruiters review résumés is what I call Three Green Lights.

The human brain likes things in sets of three.

If a recruiter sees three things that match what they are looking for, then your résumé will generally get passed on to the hiring manager. Each item they like is one Green Light.

- Title.
- Matching skill(s).
- One other item.

Of course, you cannot have any Red Lights.

You need Three Green Lights and no Red Lights, and then your résumé will be passed on to the hiring manager.

The reader can get this in 10 second or less.

Yes, this is a generalization, and not that easy in many cases, but the overall concept is true. If you provide the recruiter with what they are looking for, your résumé will get passed on.

If you do not show them the skills they are looking for now, but your résumé is easy to read, and includes something else the company looks for, then different things may happen. Your résumé might be sent to a different manager. It might be saved in the ATS (or maybe marked) so that the recruiter can find it again in the future.

Provide the recruiter what they are looking for and you will get into the go pile. Or if you have a good résumé and not what they are looking for, you have future possibilities. The key is to get the Green Lights.

You are not your résumé

One problem I have when coaching people about their résumé is that they occasionally take my comments personally.

To put it bluntly: You are not your résumé. Your résumé is not you.

The résumé is a sales document.

I understand that you may have put a lot of work into it. But if it is not working, you need to change it.

If an engineer designs a ray gun that does not fire, does he get offended when told to fix it? Or does he find ways to make it work and do what it is supposed to do?

The résumé is the same. If it does not get you interviews, then you need to do something different.

If you make the mental shift to thinking about the résumé as a sales document, you can get to the next question. What does the résumé need to say to get you an interview?

You are the product

Think of yourself as a product you are trying to sell.
- What kinds of problems does this product solve?
- What are the best things about the product?
- How do you best present those things on paper?
- How do you convince the buyer that you may have the best product, and that they should bring you in to discuss buying the product?
- What effective details can you tell them about?

How do you arrange this into a document?

How can you arrange it effectively so that people see what you want them to see, which you hope are the things they are looking for, so they will want to know more about your product?

Résumé vs. CV

Whether you use a CV (curriculum vitae) or a résumé will depend on where you live. I know there are some differences between the U.S. and other countries, and some differences among various parts of the U.S.

A résumé is a sales document. It does not contain everything you have ever done. It needs to be focused on the specifics of the position you are looking for.

A CV is a comprehensive document. It contains everything you have done. It tends to focus more on research and publications. These documents can be quite long and detailed about all the work you have accomplished.

Most positions need a résumé and not a CV. A CV is used most often for applying to positions in education or research. Some consulting companies also like to have a CV for each employee on file, to document employee experience accurately when making project proposals to their clients.

I do not have a CV for myself, because I have never applied for a position where a CV was required.

You may occasionally need a CV. Some job applications request them. It is a good idea to keep older versions of your résumé so you can pull comprehensive data from them if you need to build a CV.

Types of résumés

There are three résumé formats. Technically only two, because the third is a combination of the first two. I will describe the major types and where each might be useful.

Reverse Chronological: This is the most common type of résumé, for which you can find templates everywhere. If you are making your first résumé, an important note is that jobs are put on the résumé in reverse chronological order. The most recent is first. The oldest experience is last.

What this means is that almost everyone who reads your résumé will assume that your most recent experience is first. This also means that you do not need to put the employment dates on the left side of the document in the most visually active areas. Put the dates on the right side, right justified after the title or company, directly following those. If someone wants to look up the dates of your employment (to see how long you were at your positions) the data will be there. Then the date will not be taking up the most valuable real estate on the page.

Functional: These are often best when you are making a career change or when you have significant gaps in your résumé. If you are applying for a position where you have skills that translate well to the new position, but do not have the exact experience, this type of résumé can also be effective. This format focuses on skills or attributes not job history. There may be sections for each group of skills. Bullets under each item can describe projects worked in the past, often without mentioning the specific employer.

Often applicants will put a short and simple reverse chronological list of employers at the bottom of the résumé, but that really changes it into the type below.

Hybrid or Combination: This résumé is a combination of both types above. They often start with functional overviews to get the attention of the reader, followed by employment in (standard) reverse chronological order.

The functional aspects can be tables, short sections, or just a list of bullets. These will take a third to a half page, leaving room for positions details on the first page as well.

I think that most strong résumés fall into this final category.

Résumé writers

Résumé writers are not all created equal.

My biggest problem is that many résumé writers do not understand the hiring process, and how recruiters read résumés. I have seen plenty of résumés that look great and are quite well-written. Except that too often they are too wordy.

People who look at résumés initially just review them. They do this because they have a lot of résumés to look at, and rarely have a lot of time to do so. They do not have 10 minutes to read a résumé.

For example, if a recruiter has 100 applications for a position, and spends 10 minutes reading each résumé, that would take them two full work days. And that is if they have nothing else to do and no interruptions.

A recruiter might actually have an hour to look at that stack. That would mean 36 seconds on average per résumé. And that includes time to open the candidate in the ATS, read the cover letter (if they bother), read the résumé, accept or reject the résumé, note why the candidate is being accepted or rejected, and send the résumé on to the manager or send a rejection note. Now many of these functions are automated within the ATS, so individually those items do not take a long time, but it still leaves very little time to read the résumé.

If you are going to work with a résumé writer, find out what that person has done previously. Make sure they understand how the recruiting process works and know how to write a résumé so that a quick review will provide a positive outcome.

CHAPTER NINE: Making Your Résumé

Résumé basics

Here are the basics.

Most résumés will be submitted electronically, so the résumé needs to be named well. The name of the file should include your own name. Some people like to put in the word "résumé," or details of the version or date. Those are OK as long as you keep your name as part of the file name.

The file format should be something commonly used, like Word or PDF. If you use another format, you should consider converting it to Word or PDF before sending it out. You want the résumé to be in a format that you are confident anyone can open. Some staffing agencies do not like PDF format because they are more difficult to modify. PDF preserves format better, in case you are converting your résumé from software that companies use less commonly.

The résumé's length is worth discussing. I think you should keep your résumé to two pages at most. One is better if you can do it, but do not cram everything into one page at the expense of readability. Understand that the second page will probably never get read, just skimmed. More than two pages will increase the chance of the résumé's rejection.

Have a simple and easy-to-read layout. Make sure there is enough white space.

Use only one typeface. Use something professional, typically a serif is better than a sans-serif font. You can use something nonstandard if it is very readable, but it is usually better to stay on the conservative side. If you want to use more than one typeface, I suggest working with a graphic designer so you can choose two that work well together. Too many typefaces can make the page look gaudy or tough to read.

The smallest size you should use is 11-point, with exceptions for a header or footer.

You may use some underlining, bolding and italics if you do so conservatively, to make particularly important items stand out. If you overuse these, you will lose the effect of making priority items stand out, and will take away from the résumé's clean look. Clear and simple is best, so it is easy to read.

You should stick mostly to one color (black) unless you have reason to do otherwise, such as if you are in a profession where more color is expected. Poor use of color can distract the reader from seeing the important data you are presenting. Avoid color unless you know what you are doing.

Tables, discussed in their own later topic, can be very effective. Yes, they can get mauled by an ATS, but most ATSs now have ways to preserve the original résumé for viewing.

Graphs and charts can be highly effective if done right. For good examples of this, see *The Infographic Résumé* by Hannah Morgan (Career Sherpa).

Blocks of text

Just do not do them.

Blocks of text do not work.

I guarantee that if you write a long block of text, most recruiters will not read more than the first two lines, most often just part of the first line. (Only occasionally recruiters will skim a block of text to see if something jumps out at them.)

If anything important is in the block, it will not be seen. It will also waste space, a space that is filled but does nothing to increase the odds of getting an interview.

Simple rule: Keep all text to at most two lines. You can go over that, but each time you do, you risk that the reader will skip what you wrote.

Hiring managers are much more likely to read all the details in your résumé, unlike the recruiter, who will just skim for what they want. But keeping the text short makes the résumé more readable for those people. It keeps the ideas broken down and easier to mentally digest.

Considering that most managers do not want to read the résumés, and have a hard time finding the time to do it, you are making it easier on them. If you make it easy on them and show them what they are looking for quickly and easily, you are likely to get an interview (provided you have the correct skills, of course).

No blocks of text.

Name and contact information

Often applicants put their name in an overly large font to make it stand out. That is not important. When someone wants to know your name, or if they want your contact information or address, they know where to find it.

My own preference is to make my name slightly larger than the primary text in the résumé, and the contact information slightly smaller. I put all this information in the header, where it is often gray and therefore less noticeable. Readers then will direct their eyes to other items that you want them to see in the very limited time you have for the first visual inspection. Putting the contact information in smaller type also saves space for job-related details.

Certifications, like CPA and PMP, should be directly after your name. If they are not commonly known, they should be detailed (fully spelled out) in another part of the résumé, under either Skills or Education.

Other contact information to include:
- Your postal address.
- A phone number, noting whether home or mobile. If you have two numbers put the preferred number in bold.
- A professional email address. Using something like drunkguy@aol.com will get you rejected.

I have seen some trends recently where people leave off one or more of the items above. Or put them at the bottom instead of the top. I suggest staying with the expected; put everything where people will look for it.

Do you need to include to your LinkedIn profile? I think that it is helpful, but not required. I have never seen a candidate rejected because they did not put their LinkedIn profile address on their résumé. Usually once someone has your résumé, they will not also go look at your LinkedIn profile. If you want to include it, make it a link so it is easier to refer to.

Sections

A résumé can look cluttered and complicated. One common way to improve the overall look of the résumé is to break it into sections.

Typical sections are: Objective. Skills Overview. Work Experience. Education. The section headers are typically fully left-justified and are either bold or underlined.

Do not put section names in all capital letters. They are much more pleasant and readable in normal case.

Section headers can allow the reader to quickly and easily know what section is being read. Larger sections can be further broken down. For example, if you have worked in only one position for 25 years, you would probably have a long list of accomplishments. You could break down the list into separate parts, i.e., Project Management Accomplishments, Software Development Accomplishments, Quality Assurance Accomplishments, etc.

If you have a functional résumé, you can do the same thing. Rather than providing a long and difficult-to-scan list of skills and projects, you could (should) break it down into functional sections. The section headers alone will provide a résumé scanner a quick overview of the types of work you have done.

Subheaders are a very effective way to show a résumé skimmer the major areas where you have experience.

Brain stuff

Here is an item about how the brain works and how people read and process information.

People do not read in entire sentences. People do not read one word at a time. People read in blocks of five to seven words at a time (or four to eight, or something similar; it depends on what article was your source). This concept can be used very effectively in some places in the résumé.

- If you have a title at the top.
- If you have short bullets summarizing your skills.
- If you use an objective (which can have three sets of five to seven words).
- Each bullet under position details can be multiples of this.
- Did you see how I used an example of this?

The point is to think about how the reader is going to process the words and put the résumé in a format that is easier to process.

Objective

This is a place where I differ from the crowd.

Many résumé writers and recruiters will tell you to leave an objective off the résumé. They have countless reasons, and I will not detail them here.

My opinion is that most objectives do not work, because they do not give the readers what they are looking for. But I am in favor of ones that do. A properly written objective will provide the recruiter with what they want to see and begin to show that you are qualified for the position.

You do not need to call it an Objective. You can call it a Summary, Marketing Statement, or Executive Summary. You can just put the sentence there without attaching a section header to it.

Whatever you call it, a good objective should answer these three questions:

- What type of position are you looking for?
- What do you bring to the table, or why should they hire you over and above other candidates?
- What are you going to do for them?

Each of these three things needs to be said in five to seven words so that the entire objective is no more than one sentence. If you want someone to read the objective and for it to be effective, you need to make it short. This is what the résumé reader will see first. It is the single most important part of the résumé. You need to begin by answering those three questions.

Example:

"I am looking for a position as a Project Manager where my focused attention to detail will help the development teams to be more efficient and productive."

This is not about your personal goals. If you want to continue learning or move up into management, that is great, but this is not the place for that. Keep your personal goals in your career marketing plan. The résumé should be focused on what you are going to do for them, not what they are going to do for you.

This is a sales document. You need to sell the reader on what you are going to do for them. Once they are convinced, then you can ask for what you want. Usually that will come during or after the interview.

Sell. Sell. Sell.

Alternative Objective

I have seen this alternative to an Objective that works well. This might be called a résumé header or page title.

If you have several primary job titles that the company might look for, and you cannot summarize your title in a few words, this could work. Sometimes a title on the page can very effectively provide the reader with the information.

Project Manager * Software Engineer * Contract Manager

With a separator between the position titles, the information is very easy to scan.

After this, you still need to sell them on the other two items. What do you bring to the table, or why should they hire you over and above other candidates? What are you going to do for them?

You could do this in a simple one-line sentence, similar to the Objective but omitting the position title. Or you could use bullets as described in the next topic.

Skills Overview

After your Objective, you can provide a short and easy-to-read overview of the primary of the skills you bring. If you have used an Alternative Objective, you can use this section to finish answering the three questions listed in the previous topic.

I like to see this with short and simple bullets:
- Concise and accurate writer.
- Able to edit large volumes in a single bound.
- Immense 80,000-word vocabulary to impress clients.

If you are using this section, keep all the phrases to five to seven words. This keeps them easy to scan and ensures that they will get read.

Keep to one idea per bullet. About five bullets at most. More than that and you risk that the reader will skip some of them and continue to skim the rest of the document.

If you have more than five bullets, you could break them into two groups.

Tables (making data visually available)

Tables are a very effective way to show information. Tables are better than blocks of text, because the eyes and brain can scan a table quickly and efficiently. If a reader is looking for a particular item on your résumé, they may not find that item if it is buried in a block of text (and as previously discussed, blocks of text will most of often be skimmed or skipped).

A table could cover soft skills, hard skills or a combination. Or you can have multiple tables, if that works for your skill set.

Specific Human Resources experience includes:

Job descriptions	Behavioral interviewing	Staffing best practices
Employment branding	Job fairs	Employee retention
Candidate assessment	Applicant tracking systems	Search strategies

A table works best where there are an odd number of columns. In a résumé, generally a table will have three columns. People read from the top down and from left to right. When you make a table, the most important items should be in the upper left, the least important in the lower right.

The biggest danger with a chart like this is using words that are too commonly used in résumés and that have very little meaning like "Motivated" or "Leadership."

Using a skills overview and a table together can also be very effective. These combined with the Objective provide the Functional aspects of the résumé.

The best thing about a chart is that all the items are very visually available. It is very easy for the eyes and brain to find specific things the reader is looking for. Putting important items in tables greatly increases the chances that items will be seen. Your information is much more visually accessible, and recruiters will be able to find what they are looking for.

Formatting Work Experience

As mentioned earlier, almost all résumés that have a Work Experience section put the Work Experience in reverse chronological order. This means that the most recent experience is first, and the older experience is last. People reading your résumé will expect this. Unless you have a good reason, it is best to follow this order. If you do not follow this order, make sure that it is very clear to the reader.

Most recruiters are just going to skim your work experience, not read it. Hiring managers will generally read most of your work experience. Your job is to make it easy for either of them.

The first thing to consider is your job title and the company you worked for. You can put these on the same line or put them on separate lines. What to consider is which one to put first. In your profession, will your title or the company be more interesting or impressive? Put the more interesting one first. If they are both of interest, then they probably need to be on separate lines.

As stated previously, do not put the dates of employment on the left side. Keep them to the right, ideally right justified.

Job responsibilities. I think that most of these can be removed. The reason is that whatever your title, it is likely that most of your job responsibilities are common to everyone with the same title. The person reading the résumé will generally already know the primary responsibilities of the position. You can leave most of them off. It is a waste of space better used for other things, and you are just telling the reader what they already know.

If you feel you need to summarize your commonly known job responsibilities, then try to keep it to one line or bullet.

What is more important is to tell the reader what things you did that are different from the norm, i.e., if you are a project manager, and project managers do not generally have fiscal budget responsibilities, but you did, you should make sure that is listed as part of the job duties (and maybe in your skills table as well).

Most of your bullets (none longer than two lines) should be accomplishments, as detailed on the next topic.

Accomplishments (by the numbers)

I am sure if you have written a résumé before, you have heard this: accomplishments over responsibilities.

What is an accomplishment? Typically, anything that you can put a number on.

- Do not write out the words for the numbers.
- The numbers will stand out better if in numeric format.
- Keep each bullet point to two lines at most.
- Look on old reports to management, or performance appraisals, for example, especially if you have done many small projects.
- You do not need to list every accomplishment. Use three to six. If you have more than that, then only use those that are the most important, or alternatively, use those that are related to what you want to do next.
- If you have more accomplishments under a single position, consider breaking them into two (or more) sections, each with a more specific header.
- If you have an accomplishment, but do not know how to include it, think about how it was measured.

Example:
- Quality work: 93% two-year retention rate for placements.
- Completion of work: Filled 96% of positions when on retainer/bonus model.

To be fair, making all the bullets on your résumé into great-sounding accomplishments is probably one of the toughest parts of making a good résumé. The concepts may sound easy, but they are tough to implement well. Get help!

Accomplishments (hooks or loops)

I want to introduce yet another brain-thing to you. Looping. The concept is that the brain likes a closed loop. If something starts the brain wants an ending. Books and TV shows use this. They leave a show or chapter open-ended so that you will want to read more or wait impatiently for the next season.

People in sales call this a hook.

You can use this on your résumé. Tell the reader about an accomplishment, but do not go into all the detail about how you did it. Provide enough detail to get them interested and wanting more. Leave them wanting to know how you did it.

If they want to know more, they will bring you in for an interview, which of course is back to the purpose of the résumé: to get you in for an interview.

Keywords

Yes, keywords are important.

When you submit your résumé via an ATS, one thing the ATS will do is sort all the words that appear in the document. It will then store those against future searches.

For example, let us say that the recruiter is looking for a CAD designer who has used the Cadence package. To search on "CAD" would bring up too many résumés, so the recruiter would likely search on "Cadence." Every résumé that has that word in it will come up.

Here is the important bit: They will be ordered by the number of occurrences in the résumé. If you have the word "Cadence" in your résumé three times, your résumé will show up before everyone's résumé who has it fewer.

Yes, the most important keywords in your résumé should be included more than once. The actual number of times should depend on the importance of that keyword. The other side is that if you overuse a keyword, it can make your résumé look or sound strange.

Two or three occurrences of important keywords are plenty. Do not try to format your résumé just to fit in more keywords.

Do invisible keywords work?

For those who do not know, this would be a list of keywords at the end of a résumé. The text color is changed to white so that they cannot be seen but will be counted by an ATS or even found by a Windows search that includes content.

I do not recommend doing this.

In some cases it might work. More often the white color is stripped out by an ATS so the keyword list becomes visible, which can make the résumé look strange. And a few recruiters get annoyed by this.

Best just to put keywords as appropriate in the main sections of the résumé.

Show growth patterns

One thing that hiring managers and some recruiters like to see is a pattern of growth through your career. Whether you stayed with one company or moved through multiple companies they want to see a pattern of increasing responsibility or expertise.

The clearer you can make this progression the better.

In some cases, because of Real Life, this can be hard.

I know one person who started as an engineer. He quickly grew into a leadership role and into management.

Then he got laid off. He started his own company. Then he went back to working as an engineer, because jobs were tight, and he needed to pay the bills. Then he worked as an interim manager.

His résumé was quite confusing, because its readers could not tell whether he was an engineer or a manager. If they were looking for an engineer, they would see his management experience and think that he would not be happy as an engineer. If they were looking for a manager, they were not happy with the pattern of his experience and that he had not been doing just management recently.

In this case he was better off with two résumés, one to focus on his engineering skills and another to focus on his management skills. And still it would be difficult to show progression.

Lack of a good growth pattern is not a career destroyer, but can lead to some confusion on the résumé and make it tougher to get an interview.

Résumé gaps

Once upon a time having an employment gap in your résumé was a job killer. No one wanted to interview or hire you. The basic thought was that if you had a gap in your résumé there was something wrong with you. That there was a reason you were not employable. The specifics did not matter.

I cannot count the number of times I had managers reject my candidates because of a gap in the résumé. I would look beyond the gap or ask about it. I would find the strengths of the person and I would present that. Sometimes the manager could not see past the gap to see the potential in the candidate.

Fortunately, that attitude is less common now. Because of the dot-com crash, the telecom crash and the real estate crash, many people have gaps in their résumés. This may include the manager doing the hiring.

The other common cause of the résumé gap is the need to take off time to care for a sick or elderly family member. People are more understanding of this now, because it occurs more frequently.

It can still be tough getting back into the job market if you are coming off one of those gaps. You still need to have a good explanation for the gap.

As I have said before, you need to be able to explain it in positive terms. You can do this by explaining what you were doing during that time. "I took some time off to care for my elderly mother" or "There was no market for my previous skills, so I spent the time picking up new ones."

The point here is to show that you were doing something productive. Lack of a good explanation can come across as negative to interviewers, which could affect your chances of getting a job offer.

You may be able to shield a smaller gap in your résumé, such as one caused by time in a job search, by showing employment dates only in years instead of years and months.

Résumés and discrimination

Discrimination is a real problem. I do not have a solution for you. Instead I will give you a choice.

Do you put items in your résumé that might cause you to be rejected because of discrimination?

Do you include the date of your college graduation? Do you include that you are a volunteer treasurer for an LGBTQ group? Do you include that you are a member of the Society for Black Engineers?

The problem is that you do not know what type of discrimination you may run into. There may be a company that discriminates. Or there may be a great company with one person who discriminates. If you put this information on your résumé, that one person could block you from getting a job you could love.

If you leave it off your résumé you could run into the problem in a different way. You go to an interview and as soon as you are there you get rejected for a discriminatory reason (though that would never be admitted).

The choice is up to you. Are you going to include that information on your résumé?

If you do, it could get you rejected early. This might be a good thing. If a company is going to discriminate it is better that they do it up front and not waste your time with an interview. Or it might be bad, because one bad apple could ruin your chance to work for a great company. If you do not include it in your résumé you would still get rejected from a company that discriminates, just during the interview process.

Historically my suggestion has been to include this information on your résumé. If you get brought in for an interview you can be pretty sure that it is not a discriminatory company. If you get rejected, it might be because of discrimination or it might be because of other reasons. In some cases, it might help. Police forces often look to recruit minorities to create a more diverse workforce, for example.

If you have not read the Discrimination topic in Chapter Eleven, you can get more of my thoughts there. There is no best answer for this, because it is very much situational. What do you choose?

Try to avoid awards related to federal protected classes (race, color, religion, national origin, sex, age or disability) unless they are directly related to the position you are seeking.

Personal information

I was a software engineer. After having been laid off, I saw an ad in the employment section of a newspaper from a small company looking for a software engineer. That same small agency was looking for a recruiter.

I faxed over a résumé and a cover letter. In the cover letter I mentioned that I was interested in the software engineer position, but that I would also like to hear about the recruiter position. The owner of the company, who reviewed all incoming faxes, brought me in for an interview for the recruiter position.

After the interview he was concerned that I was too quiet. He saw on my résumé that I was a mobile DJ and decided to continue the conversation in a second interview. One year later, I was leading the group in placements.

I did not list DJ under Employment. I listed it under Interests. If I had not put that on my résumé, I would not have secured the job. I would not be writing this book.

My lesson from this is that items of personal interest or hobbies can make a difference. They can show traits and characteristics that might not otherwise be visible on the résumé. They can also give interviewers something interesting to talk about that is not related to the position, which can help to break the ice and relieve interview tensions.

You can put a single line at the end of your résumé:

Interests: Writing, racquetball, game collecting.

Avoid items related to Section VII protected discrimination areas. Avoid controversial topics. For example, I am a Boston Red Sox fan. If the reviewer was a Yankees fan, my résumé might get tossed.

Most recruiters will tell you to keep personal information off the résumé. I think that careful use of personal information, like interests and hobbies, can help you in the job seeking process.

Awards, Education, final notes

A few last comments about résumés.

Old experience. Yes, it is common to cut out or summarize older experience. My personal preference is to summarize it. Opinions vary, but it is OK to cut out experience older than 15 to 20 years.

Awards. Include awards related to the job you are seeking or that provide information about your character that you want to convey to the hiring manager. Include the dates. This will let the reader know whether the item is recent and relevant. If you leave off the date, then people will assume the item is old. Place older items near the end of the résumé, before or after Education.

Education. Unless you are a recent graduate, the actual courses you took in college should be removed from your résumé. Your education can be summarized. Your GPA should be on the résumé if it was 3.0 or higher, but again, once you are a few years out of college you can remove this. Your actual work experience is more important. If you have any completed college education, then you should remove your high school education.

If you have a partial college education, my preference is that you include this, e.g., you completed 85 percent of your requirements toward a Bachelor of Science in Computer Science. This can be important when interviewers consider how much theory a person knows. If you have a college degree not related to a job you are applying for, you should keep this on your résumé. Showing you completed college provides evidence that you can finish what you start.

Do not include your references in your résumé. Have them in a separate document.

Spell check and proofread the résumé many times and have at least two or three other people proof it. Spelling mistakes can get you rejected quickly.

CHAPTER TEN: HR and How Companies Work

A day in the life of an HR person

Working as an external recruiter I often hear complaints about HR and how they never respond or respond too slowly. I have even heard complaints that HR is dysfunctional. I find much of this criticism to be unreasonable.

I have formal HR training (SPHR) and have worked several positions that include internal HR work. Most important is that I am in contact with HR people on a daily basis.

I think that many people lack an understanding of what an HR person does every day.

Your average HR person could be involved in: Labor and Employee Relations, Training and Development, Rewards (benefits, compensation, etc.), Risk Management, Workforce Planning and Employment, Strategic HR Management (if the company is reasonably progressive), Compliance and Reporting (the number of laws related to HR increases every year).

Most HR departments are understaffed. The ratios of HR to the rest of the company are smaller than they have ever been. Many companies consider HR to be overhead and keep the department as small as possible.

The pace of recruiting is often inconsistent. Sometimes there is no recruiting and sometimes there are bursts of hiring. On top of all the work listed above, and being understaffed, they do recruiting in what amounts to their spare time.

Many of the HR people I know work 50 to 60 hours per week and still cannot get done everything that needs to get done.

Sometimes they do not get back to you because they are waiting for the hiring manager to get back to them.

What do you do with this information? Be patient and respectful. If you have not heard back from the HR person wait a week to contact them again. Always be respectful of their time. While the hiring process may still move slowly, treating the HR person well will improve your chances in the process. Being impatient and disrespectful will reduce your chances.

How to annoy a recruiter

I had been working on some telecommute positions that were getting me quite a few applicants on a national level. Over the course of seven days, the posting had more than 1,000 hits, and I had received at least 120 résumés.

Unfortunately, about two-thirds of the applicants did not tell me which of the four positions they were interested in. I was forced to do a presort of the applicants before I could look at them for each position.

I was quite surprised to open one résumé file to have it say "Sorry no résumé is available. I will furnish one if invited to an interview. Thank you."

Not only did the applicant not tell me which position interested them, but left me no way to determine whether the person was even qualified for an interview.

Given that I had another 119 applicants for the position, there was really no reason for me to spend any more time on the applicant. The résumé immediately went to the "No Interest" folder.

To be blunt, the candidate annoyed me. The person wasted my time. This applicant did the exact opposite of what an applicant should try to do. He knocked himself out of the process immediately.

The point of the résumé is to get the recruiter interested enough to want to do an interview, to want to spend more time with you.

What can you take away from this story?
- Do not waste the time of the recruiter.
- Provide the recruiter with the proper information.
- Do not present the recruiter with an attitude that will get you rejected.
- Do not expect more than you have earned (getting an interview without a résumé).

To put another way; respect the time of the recruiter. Respect the time and effort of every person you meet on your job search, and it will greatly improve your chances of success.

Not our job

It is not our job to read your entire résumé.

The job of HR people and recruiters is to find a person to fit an open position who can do the job well.

If a résumé is poorly made and gets passed over, the recruiter does not care, providing they can find a good person for the position.

We do not have the time or interest to read a long and wordy résumé. Most recruiters feel this way. Let me be really clear about the underlying assumptions that are never spoken:

- If you have a good résumé, you are a good candidate.
- If you have a poor résumé, you are a poor candidate.
- If your résumé is easy to read and quickly shows the relevant skills to the recruiter then you are a good candidate and probably a good communicator.
- If your résumé has even one spelling mistake, is poorly formatted, too wordy, too much text, too long or too confusing, you will be considered a poor candidate with poor communication skills.

While these are not true for all candidates it does not really matter.

Take the time to make a quality résumé. It is worth it.

Priority of recruiting

One of the problems with a job search is that human resources and recruiting often do not have a high priority in many companies. People in HR have more responsibilities than ever, while their proportional numbers are not growing.

In smaller companies HR often reports to finance. In larger companies HR is often part of operations. Seldom does HR have its own C-level executive. What this means is that HR is often undervalued and understaffed.

What does this mean to you in your job search? It means that company response might be slow. The hiring process might be slow. It might mean that no matter how good you are, or how good your connections are, you might be unable to influence the process to move better or more quickly.

It means that you need to be respectful of the time of people in human resources. They are swamped. The last thing they need is an irate candidate wanting to know the status of their application.

The good news is that this is improving. More companies are starting to understand the value of HR, and equally, the value of a strong staffing process. Some companies really are putting their people first.

I once worked on an on-site contract for a not-for-profit agency. It was quite different work for me, and it was exceptionally difficult to find good people for what they were able to pay. What was great was that HR reported to organizational development. OD was focused on the best way to build the organization. It was an amazing people focus which made it a great experience despite the low pay and difficult work.

The next takeaway from this topic is to pay attention to the quality of the staffing process. If the process is abnormally slow, it might mean that the company does not prioritize people. If the process is great, it probably means that the company values people and the recruiting process, which in turn probably means that it will be a good place to work.

Hiring process

What should you expect?

After applying, you should get at least some acknowledgment from a company within a few days of applying for a position. This process is now mostly automated.

Within about a week, your application should be reviewed. You should be sent a rejection, or the application should be forwarded to the hiring manager (though you will not be told if this happens, so sometimes no news is good news).

You can expect the hiring manager to take up to a week to get back to HR. (And if they do not, HR people will often track them down to get responses, if they have time.) Once your application has been reviewed by the hiring manager, you will get a rejection from HR, or be contacted by HR quickly for an interview. The initial interview setup can take a few days.

The next step will depend on the process of the company. Some companies like HR to do an initial phone screen. In some companies the hiring manager, or someone in their team, will do a phone screen. Some will bring you in for a single in-person interview. Other companies will break the interview process down into multiple in-person interviews, in an effort to reduce overall time spent by the interview team. If a company requires more than two in-person interviews, there may be a problem, though I have seen cases where applicants had five interviews and still got hired.

After a completed interview process, the team generally meets within two days to make a decision on the candidate. If many interviews are under way, the team may not meet until all scheduled interviews are completed, sometimes up to a week after the first one.

The worst case here is if you are a "maybe" candidate. The team does not want to reject you but is hoping to get a candidate who is a better fit. The company will not tell you that you fall into this category. It will just tell you that it is still interviewing.

If the team likes you for the job, an offer will be generated in a week or less, sometimes a few days.

If you add this up, the time to hire, starting from the time you apply, can be three to eight weeks. This, unfortunately, is normal. If it goes faster, that tells you something positive about the company.

Fastest hire I have seen recently: I interviewed the candidate on a Tuesday. I sent the résumé to my client on Wednesday. They interviewed the candidate on Friday and emailed him an offer on Saturday. On Sunday he accepted. Five days.

Slowest hire: Candidate interviewed and submitted in December. Hired in May. Six months.

There are a lot of companies with a poor or slow hiring process. I do not think it is something that should deter you from going through the process. It is only one aspect of the company. There will be many other considerations.

Finding a contact in a company

Who do you try to contact once you have applied?

Most of the companies I work with are either small or medium-size, which means that they are not big enough to have continual recruiting needs. Sometimes they are not big enough even to have a full-time person working in HR.

A larger company generally hires more consistently over the course of a year (providing the company is growing, of course). A larger company is more likely to have people dedicated to recruiting.

The difficulty here is determining which person on the team is responsible for the position that interests you. It is generally worth calling and asking for a recruiter, and when you get the person's voicemail (which is fairly likely, because people do not often answer their phones anymore), leave a polite message with the person stating your name, number and the position you are interested in. Ask for the status of your application, or for the message to be forwarded to the appropriate recruiter if you reached the wrong person. (Most larger companies have voicemail systems that allow messages to be forwarded.)

If you are contacting a medium-size company, it is unlikely to have people specializing in recruiting. It will have an HR generalist (or sometimes an office manager or accountant who does part-time HR) who does recruiting on top of the rest of their work. You will generally be able to leave them a message.

A smaller company, (depending on its actual size) will probably not have an HR person, so you may need to leave a message with a receptionist or office manager.

If you happen to know the name of the hiring manager, you can contact that person directly.

If you get a live person or voicemail, your message should be the same. Introduce yourself. Provide the name of the position you applied to, ask for a status update, and slowly and clearly leave your phone number — twice. Be polite and respectful and quick.

Once you have had an interview, the rules will change somewhat, as discussed in a later topic

Broken hiring process

Mark found a job that greatly interested him. He received the direct contact information for the hiring manager from a friend. He contacted the manager and received a response within 24 hours. Later that week he did a phone interview with the manager, and it went very well. The manager asked Mark to go through the online application process, which Mark did, with some difficulty. Once the manager was able to see the application, Mark was invited in for a second, face-to-face interview. It also went very well, and the manager told Mark that he would be getting a job offer.

Then the problems began. It took over a week for Mark to receive the offer. Then when he started to go through the tasks required in the offer letter, he found that HR did not even know that he has been sent the offer letter. It took

over a week for Mark to get that one settled. At the same time, he was interested in getting benefits details so that he could determine his total compensation for the position. That took a while. He had to wait for the drug test result before he could resign from his current position. Overall, it took two months from the time that Mark got contact with the manager to the day he started the job.

And this is not even the worst example. I had one client that had a candidate in for interviews five different times over the course of a month. Even when those went well, there were other items to negotiate. It took about three months before he was able to start the job.

At least in these two cases it worked. Sometimes it does not work.

Sometimes the hiring process is broken.

Do not take it personally. Know that it is not your fault.

If you are interested in the job, you may have to jump through flaming hoops many times.

Know this also: A broken hiring process does not mean it is a bad company. Sometimes it is a great company with great jobs but a poor hiring process.

You may have to decide whether you want to endure the paperwork and setbacks of an outrageous process or move on.

CHAPTER ELEVEN: The Search

Discrimination in your job search? Just move on.

Do job seekers run into discrimination? Absolutely.
Is it legal? No.
Is it worth fighting over while conducting a job search? NO!
I am not saying that discrimination is acceptable. I am saying not to dig holes where you know there is no treasure. If you know a company discriminates based on any category, then walk away. Look for a company that will treat you well. Look for a company that searches for, and hires people, based on what they can accomplish.

Let me suggest another viewpoint: In the coming years as talent gets harder to find, which companies are going to grow and thrive? Those that discriminate and limit their talent pool? Or those that embrace diversity?

If you run into a company that discriminates you should walk away. And tell others so that they will not waste their time and can walk away also. Leave the company to die a cold and lonely death. Would you want to work at a company that discriminates? Would you be happy there? Would you want to be fighting a battle just to be able to do your job?

I have done this as a consultant. I have walked away from companies that have discriminatory hiring practices. I do not want to work for companies like that and I certainly cannot sell them to my candidates.

There are a lot of great companies out there. There are companies that care about their people. Work hard to find one. Find your treasure and thrive.

Respect

Pay attention to how people treat you.
There are companies that will treat you like a number through the application process. If that is how you are treated then, you can often take that as the way that you might be treated as an employee.

Some companies will treat you with disrespect. You do not need to put up with that. You do not need to fight about it, or even tell them what they are doing wrong. Plenty of good companies treat people well.

If you are not respected move on. Do not dwell on it. Keep looking for those good companies. They are out there.

In the course of your job search, treat every person you meet with respect.

Respect and disrespect both cause ripples.

Being disrespectful to a receptionist at an interview can cause you to get rejected.

Being respectful to cleaning staff can earn you an extra interview.

Be respectful about places where you worked and people you worked with, even if you think you have reason not to be. Being disrespectful and unprofessional about past jobs and people will have you out the door before you can say "rejected."

I have seen these things happen.

You deserve respect.

Every person you meet in your job search deserves respect.

Finding jobs (overview)

What is the best way to find out about jobs?

Your network: This method is still the best way to find new jobs and has been the best for many years. Tell your friends and contacts that you are looking for something new. You can ask people whether there are any jobs where they work, or whether they know of any other open positions that are similar.

However, there are many, many sources for new jobs, and you should not restrict yourself to any one method. Here are more thoughts about that:

Change the signature file for your email to include a line about a job search. It does not need to be anything fancy. Something like "Looking for my next exciting software development opportunity." This way every email you send is another message to people that you are looking for something new.

If you do not have a LinkedIn account, you should probably make one. This is the single most-used online tool. You can use it to stay connected with people and look up job postings. Note that job postings can come in many forms here: updates from connections, postings in groups, and the LinkedIn job listings.

Agencies and headhunters. The biggest advantages of these are that they often know about positions that are not posted anywhere else. You may also find duplication among agencies with the jobs they are posting.

I do still see jobs printed in the newspaper on occasion, but not often. It is worth looking in the Sunday paper jobs section, but for most jobs I would not count on finding much. Most newspapers now have their job sections online so for many this may be an easier option.

See also separate topics about:
- Groups.
- Job boards and job aggregators.
- Working with an agency (many topics in a separate chapter).

Groups (more ways to find jobs)

More ways to find out about jobs.

Job search groups: Depending on the population of the location where you live, you may be able to join job search groups. These are frequently started and run by an individual and have stayed around long past the time the founder started a new job. Often the founder stays involved to keep the group going and to help people. Most of the members of these types of groups keep changing as new people become unemployed and those in the group find jobs. These are great places to get help, get leads, and help others in the same situation you are in.

Local online networking groups: Many of these started in the same way as the in-person groups, but over time the people stayed in touch online by starting a Yahoo, LinkedIn, Google or Facebook group. These groups tend to get larger over time, often getting thousands of members. One of the biggest advantages of a group like this is that while most of the members started out unemployed, most stay in the group to help once they are employed again. They become a great place to connect with people from a variety of companies. Members often provide links to new jobs, job leads, and sometimes opportunities to meet and talk in-person about your job search.

Specialized professional groups: Almost every profession has specialized groups. These are groups that meet to discuss their profession, often have monthly meetings with speakers and presentations, and are also great places to network. My area has three different HR groups (two of which are divisions of national organizations) and at least a dozen very specific groups for computer professionals. If you are not already a member of a professional group, join one. And stay connected after you find a new job.

LinkedIn groups. When LinkedIn started, it also started its groups. These were a great way to connect with people in your profession, your hobby or others who were looking for a job. The most common problem is keeping up with the volume, especially if you have a lot of connections (and so a swamped primary feed) and are in many groups. If you are actively looking for a job, look to see if there are any groups in your location or specialty, join the group(s), and make it part of your daily job search activity to keep up with the groups.

Live networking groups: There are many groups founded just to be networking groups, that do not have a specialty or focus. Something these are funded by a local Chamber of Commerce to promote local networking, or sometimes by socially active companies. Some groups may not relate specifically to a lot of jobs that fit your profession, but they are a great place to meet people, expand your network and practice networking.

State and federal agencies: Department of Labor, Workforce Development, or those of many other names, depending on where you live. These are government-funded agencies that exist to help people find employment. If you have a local agency, and are not employed, investigate this immediately. They typically provide a wide variety of services including interview preparation, help with your résumé, job search groups and coaches, speakers, presentations and more. Free to the unemployed.

Job boards and job aggregators, oh my

Once upon a time job boards were touted as THE way to find a new job. They were quite popular with companies and candidates both. There were many options for candidates. You could search for jobs and apply. You could also post your résumé and make it public. You could set up notifications for specific types of jobs. You could even block specific companies from seeing your résumé (like your current employer). The three biggest were Monster, CareerBuilder, and Dice, though there were many others.

These started to lose popularity with the advent of job aggregators. These would search the web for jobs at any company and repost them all to their own site. Because of these many companies found that they could skip using the paid job sites and still get more applicants for their positions. Indeed, SimplyHired and ZipRecruiter are a few of these.

The aggregators allowed companies to pay for sponsored ads that would put them at the top of the list and get more candidate exposure. Over time the aggregators got bigger, and other problems started to show up. Sometimes jobs were repeated many times. Sometimes jobs came up that were old and no longer available. These sites are constantly working on these problems, but they are not gone. It can still take quite some time to get through the long lists of available jobs, many of which may not fit what you were searching for. There are also options for posting your résumé, but these do not seem to be used as much as searching for positions.

The original job boards are still around. They do not have as many jobs as they had at their peak. Candidates do not seem to use them as much, though it is still worth your time to check their jobs on a regular basis. The job aggregators generally get significantly more traffic, because they have a higher volume of jobs.

Specialized sites: There are also hundreds of specialized national job sites for specific professions. For example, Engineering.com has a place to post engineering jobs for free. These may have some local jobs, and if you are willing to relocate will likely have a good number of jobs in new locations.

Plenty of options are available to keep any job searcher occupied for quite a long time.

Search agents

Every major job board, and probably most of the minor boards, have job search agents. When you create an account on the job board, you can set up search agents that will automatically notify you when jobs are posited that fit your criteria.

If it is worth using a site, if you go to that site to search for jobs, it is worth setting up a search agent. This can save you hours of time every week. Rather than having to search each site manually, you can be notified via email or text every time the right type of position shows up.

You might need to put in multiple search strings because of differing titles, e.g., if you are a software engineer, you might get notified on jobs with the titles "Software Engineer," "Software Developer," "Java Developer," "Full Stack Developer," etc.

The downside of this is that you are going to get a lot more email, and regardless of what you put into the search string, you will get jobs that do not interest you.

One of the best points is that you can turn these off at any time and you should stop getting notifications.

Extra hint: Agency recruiters do this. They set up agents to notify them when new positions arrive, so that they can call the company, get a contract and work on the positions.

Posted job requirements

You do not have all the qualifications listed in the online job description. What should you do?

Job descriptions are generally written around the ideal candidate. They include every skill that the hiring team might want a candidate to have. They are long and detailed.

The reality is that companies almost never hire someone who is an exact fit as shown by the job description. Most positions are filled by people who simply can do the job.

Look at the job description. Even if you do not have everything on the list, can you do the job? If yes, they apply.

A problem with a long job description is that it is sometimes difficult to determine what the most important skills are. Recruiters have a way to get this information. When we meet the hiring manager we ask, "What are the three most important skills needed to do this job?" Sometimes there are more than three skills, but the point is that the long job description has been narrowed to the most important skills. Obviously as a job applicant you will not have access to the hiring manager to ask this question. But you can still look at the job description and try to extract the most important points.

If you can perform the primary tasks required of the positions, then apply.

There may be unusual cases. Like an entry level job that requires a Ph.D. People who are just out of school with a Ph.D. need jobs, too. And of course some jobs do require a Ph.D. Sure, some job descriptions sound strange, but most likely there are good reasons for those things that sound unusual.

Some job descriptions have impossible requirements. When the C# programming language was about two years old, I remember seeing some job descriptions that required five years of experience with C#. Job descriptions like these tend to scare people away. It sounds as if the company does not know what it is doing. For some applicants, maybe you, the situation might also be an opportunity to get in the door and educate the company. If you apply and do not get the job, then at least you took a chance.

One final note: If you see a job description looking for a Super Star (yes, it's in the job description) you may want to be cautious, as the company may have unrealistic expectations.

Bad job postings

I am sure that every job seeker gets frustrated looking at most of the job postings that are out there. They are often quite long and have a very long list of required skills.

They can be depressing to look at. The number of people that meet all the job requirements is often very small. The worst part of this is that some people will not apply, even if they probably can do the job.

Agencies and headhunters are often better at this. They will talk with the hiring manager to find out what is most important in the job and can put out a posting that contains only those skills. But often time is limited, and it is easier just to paste the client's job description to the agency site (minus the company name, etc.). I know because I have done this myself.

Some job postings are starting to separate required skills from optional or bonus skills.

In the ideal world, there would be both an internal and external job description. The internal one would describe all the skills the ideal person would have as well as the overall responsibilities and goals. The external one would talk about the cool aspects of the company and why you would want to work there, and then (once you have become interested) tell you the most important skills required for the position.

I like to write interesting job descriptions (which I really call job ads), and I have come up with some that are effective as well. But I will say, yet again, that HR will not likely have time to do things like this. On rare occasions you will see that HR has worked with marketing to come up with some good job advertisements.

You can probably expect job descriptions to be too long and detailed until companies figure out that HR needs to be better staffed and empowered.

Applying online

Answering some of the most common questions about applying online for jobs:

Do you need to put in your Social Security number if you are asked for it? No. Your Social Security number is needed for a background or credit check. The company should not be doing these without your explicit permission. You can provide your number when you are signing a form to give permission to do one of these checks. Get a copy of the form.

As already discussed, it is now illegal in many states to ask for your salary history. Many corporations that operate in multiple states are removing this from their online application even if some of their states do not yet have a law against it. It is just easier for them to operate that way. I think you will see still more companies getting away from asking for salary history as part of the application.

It is not illegal to ask for your target salary. You have a choice of tactics here:

- Enter the number at the top of your range. Many people expect that the company will try to argue you down, so they like to start with the higher number. This tends to create more rejections for salary. Also, if your number is at the high end of the range for the employer, they will tend to have higher expectations if they interview you.
- Enter a number in the middle of your range. This has less chance of getting you immediately rejected for having a salary that is too high, at least getting you in for an interview so that you can prove your worth. You may have to be more persistent if the company tries to get you to accept a lower number.

- If you are working with an external recruiter who tells you to apply online for the position, you should have discussed the salary range with that person already, and the recruiter can tell you the best number to enter.

Different ways to apply

Finding a creative way to apply may be a way into your next job.

If you know the name of the manager, you can mail a résumé directly to that person. Managers almost never get direct mail anymore, so sending a physical résumé with cover letter might get some attention.

You could send your résumé with a box of donut holes and a message "I can fill the hole in your engineering team!""

The point is to do something interesting, but not extravagant, that gets attention.

Stopping by to apply

Once upon a time if a company had a job opening you could take your résumé and go there. You could get an application from the receptionist and fill it out right there. You could then hand the application and résumé to the receptionist.

That is how most people applied for jobs.

Recently in an online discussion about this, someone was asking if he should stop by at the company and drop off a résumé. My response was of course he should stop by.

Many of the other responses were that he should not stop by, that he should follow the normal online application process. Many of the responses were quite emphatic about this. Some even said that by not following the rules you were likely to have your application thrown out.

I was surprised by this, so I did a quick poll among some of the HR people I know. Some thought that it was proactive; others thought it was poor behavior. Here is what made the difference: age. The HR people who were older tended to think that it was OK to stop by; the younger people often considered it to be entitled behavior.

Aside from finding this a cool reversal of many of the common opinions of millennials, I was not sure what to tell the person who posted the original question.

When I am working on-site with a client, if a candidate shows up at the front door with a résumé, if I am available, I will go to briefly meet the candidate in person. I think this is a proactive move by the applicant, and I think it should be rewarded with personal contact if possible. This says something good about the applicant, and it improves the odds that I will recommend an in-person interview with the hiring manager.

Clearly not everyone agrees with me. I think my recommendation on this one would be on the conservative side. Follow the application guidelines that are posted online. If you are a little more gutsy and want to take the chance that your résumé will get thrown out, but increase your odds of an interview if it is not thrown out, then apply in person.

Regardless of what you do for this, you should still attempt to connect personally with anyone that you know at the company. That is the best way to improve your odds.

Internal referrals

I cannot count the number of times I have told people this one:

Internal referrals are the best way to find a new job.

Again. Internal referrals are the best way to find a new job.

If you know someone in a company, apply online if necessary, but also send your résumé directly to people you know, especially if some of them have hiring authority.

Qualifier: If the company has a paid internal referral program, send your résumé only to your best contact, and do not apply online until your contact suggests that you do so. To send to multiple people in the company or apply online first may jeopardize the fee that your primary contact could collect. In some cases, you will have to apply online but also mention the name of your contact in the application.

It comes down to this: Internal referrals are the most productive employees with the least turnover.

HR knows this. Internal recruiters (or HR people tasked with recruiting) will generally put internal referrals on the top of the pile.

They will be the first sent to the hiring manager. They will be interviewed first.

Even if the company has a great paid internal referral program, this is the best and cheapest way for them to recruit well-qualified people.

It is the most effective method you can have for finding a new job. It is not wrong to go around the online application for your first contact. Most companies know and expect this. It works and is the best for everyone involved.

Posting your résumé

Should you post your résumé online?

I think that this depends on the details of your search.

If your search is urgent, you are out of a job and need money to eat and pay the rent, then yes.

If you are looking to relocate, then probably. Finding contacts and positions in remote locations can be more difficult and posting your resume might open new opportunities.

Things to consider:

- If you are employed, make sure that the site you are considering gives you the option to make your résumé public or not, and gives the option of blocking companies, including your current employer.
- Some sites allow companies that buy into the database to get your contact information and contact you directly. Others make the company go through their own contact system, which can be better if you like privacy and like to keep your personal information more secure. My recommendation is that you post your résumé only at sites where you know your personal information is secure.
- Make sure you post your target location. Regardless of what location you post, you will likely get messages from recruiters in other locations.
- Anytime you post your résumé, you will get queries about jobs that do not interest you, and sometimes

jobs for which you are not qualified. This is part of the price you pay for having more opportunity.
- Job boards that are more specific to your industry are more likely to get you jobs that are the type of position that you are looking for.

Years ago, I made an email address that I was using specifically for a job search for myself. Thirteen years later I am still getting emails on that address (mostly spam). Posting your résumé online may get you more opportunities, but it will also get you more junk email to deal with.

What is an ATS?

An Applicant Tracking System (ATS) is a software package used by companies to track candidates through the hiring process. Companies will often buy or lease ATS software once they get big enough, or have enough open positions, that they cannot track the candidates adequately with spreadsheets. Most smaller companies will not use an ATS.

Frequently the ATS is now a website that people from the company log into, rather than an installed software package that can be more difficult to maintain. These packages are generally integrated with the company website (or the company website is linked to the ATS website) and are linked to the email addresses of all related employees in the hiring process.

How does an ATS work? The first thing to understand is that they are centered around jobs. Nothing happens in the ATS without a job. Whatever the approval process of a company for open positions, the jobs will get entered into the ATS and frequently posted from there as well.

When you apply, and your application goes into a queue for a job, your application patiently waits there until someone reviews it. There is no ATS black hole. Your résumé cannot get lost in the ATS. Your application will wait in the ATS until the person assigned to review applications for that position rejects it or sends it to the hiring manager.

If you have not heard from the company, it means that HR has likely not gotten to your application yet, because HR probably is understaffed, or because the application is sitting in the queue of the hiring manager. The hiring manager may not understand that hiring should be a priority, and that it is important to get back to candidates (in which case HR is probably pounding on the door to remind the manager to spend some time in the ATS). Or it just means the company has a poor hiring process.

The overall point here is that the ATS is just software. It is the people who are responsible for running the hiring process. Sometimes the ATS makes this easy, sometimes harder.

In theory, once you apply for a position, your résumé could be reviewed for other positions that open. This is the entire reason why the résumé is scanned and broken down into a word list for keyword searching (as the search engines do). The problem is that companies seldom use this capability. Again, this comes back to available time. Doing a simple search for previous candidates in an ATS is easy. But taking that list and contacting people about their interest and availability is a time-consuming task. It just does not get done very often, which is why it is good to track your target companies and reapply when new positions show up.

Mind you, it does not bother me that companies do not have time for this. If they did, staffing agencies would have a whole lot less work.

ATS problems

The ATS is often viewed as the source of problems in the hiring process. No. The ATS is not the problem. The problem is that HR does not often have the staff or funding to properly use the ATS.

As an example, I worked on an on-site recruiting contract for a small manufacturing company. One of my first projects was to deal with applicants in the ATS. Since the recruiting position had been open for six months, that meant that I had to respond to candidates who had applied six months earlier!

I cringed. Some candidates I needed to reject. I was not happy at sending a rejection for a six-month-old application, but that was better than not sending one at all. Some of the applicants were good. To those I had to send messages asking if they were still available. Not fun.

The problem was not the ATS, but the lack of someone to respond to applicants.

ATS software has some lesser problems. There are hundreds, maybe thousands, of applications. Each has different capabilities. From the applicant perspective, some are better than others.

Why do people have to manually enter their work experience (and other résumé data) after uploading their résumé? In most cases the reason is so that the ATS can present a consistent format to the hiring manager. In theory this makes it easier for that person to review the candidates. Some of the better ATS packages will scan the original résumé and populate the job history section so that you do not need to do that manually. Then they allow you to edit what they put together. My experience is that most hiring managers ignore most of this and just look at the résumé.

The best thing you can do is follow the ATS instructions as best you can. This does not guarantee that you will get an interview, but at least it will not knock you out of the process. Skipping parts of the process, or thinking that you can go around them, might get you rejected.

Social media

Social media. I am not going to dig too deep into this topic. Odds are high that whatever I write will be different in a few years. This page is just an overview.

Should you use social media in your job search?

Yes. Any method of looking for a new position is worth trying and could work for you.

I have heard of people getting jobs via Twitter, Facebook, Instagram, and more.

I post updates to LinkedIn that automatically post to Twitter. I do not generally post to Facebook. Why? I post to sites that work for me, and for the types of people whom I place. I post to sites that help me to find the right people for the positions I am looking to fill.

The key is to try different sites and determine what works for your own career path, and for the companies that you would like to work for.

LinkedIn is covered in separate topics. For most job searchers, using LinkedIn is a must.

A word of caution: Social media issues go both ways. Things said and done online are difficult to erase. Whatever you do on social media, remember that what you write, send or post could be around for an indefinite time. People have lost jobs because of emails, tweets and Facebook postings.

My suggestion is to keep the personal parts of your life personal. Posting your negative opinions online is not personal. Do not post anything that could be detrimental to your career, or to the career of any other person you know. Do not say negative things about companies or people, regardless of how you feel. Never. Ever.

Branding

You need to create your personal brand! You must let people know who you are, what you can do, and what you stand for!

Eh. Maybe. If you are applying for a position as a Social Media Engagement Professional, then you better have an amazing brand and online presence.

If you are a mechanical engineer, maybe not so much.

When you read about personal branding, usually it is really about what you are doing to market yourself. What are you doing so that people will know what you do, and that you are looking for a new position?

I think a better term for this is inbound marketing. What do you do to get people to call you?

- In the signature file in your personal email, include a line like "Looking for my next mechanical engineering adventure," or "Looking to solve new mechanical engineering problems in warehouse logistics." That way every time you send an email, to anyone, you are letting them know that you are looking.
- Share jobs to your network. When you find positions that do not fit you, you can gain public credibility and status by posting positions to people whom you know, or to groups that you are in. And in your signature is something about the position that you are looking for.
- Help people. If you are part of online or in-person groups, be willing to share your own job search secrets. Helping others will come back to you.

In addition, you can do things to show that you are a Subject Matter Expert (SME).

- Write articles about things that you have done that can help others in your field.
- Volunteer to work for not-for-profits doing what you do best.
- If you are experienced, mentor others in your field.

Another way to view this is that you are constantly doing activities that help to sell yourself.

The black hole

You apply to a job online. You go to the website, upload your résumé, fill out the application and hit Send.

Then you hear nothing back.

And hear nothing.

And hear nothing.

And you check and the job is still there.

You try to apply again, and it tells you that you have already applied.

What can you do? It seems as if you just sent your résumé into a black hole never to return.

You check the job listing and there is no one to contact. No names or phone numbers.

What next? Here are a few things to try:

- Contact someone you know in the company. Use LinkedIn to find people whom you might know from past jobs. (You could have done that before you applied ... but that is another topic.) Ask the person to check with HR or find out if they know the hiring manager.
- Look up the company phone number. Call and ask for HR or ask for the person in HR who does recruiting for the position you applied for. If you can reach a receptionist, you have good odds of being connected to someone who does something hiring-related. Odds are also good that the person will not answer the phone. Be sure to leave a clear message. Say your name clearly and your phone number (twice

even). Mention which position you applied for and ask for the status of your application. Let them know you appreciate their time and hope to hear back.

Understand that the person you left a message with is probably swamped and does not have much time for returning messages. Leaving a courteous and respectful message will greatly increase the odds that you will get called back.

Guaranteed success? No. But this attempt will give you better odds than something returning from a black hole.

Following up to an application

You are interested in a company, and it requires that you apply online. How do you follow up after the application?

When you apply for the job, most automated systems (Applicant Tracking Systems) will respond with an email telling you that you are in the system. Usually the next step is for someone in HR to review the application and résumé and determine whether to send the application to the hiring manager. If the company is large enough, a dedicated recruiter will do the review. In some companies the hiring manager does the initial review. If they like your application, they will typically contact you within about two weeks of applying.

How do you follow up before that?

If you know someone in the company, your best bet is to contact that person and ask them the name of the correct person to contact. Sometimes you can use LinkedIn to find the name of the proper contact. Sometimes if you call in you can be directed to the correct person. Sometimes the best method is to walk in the front door and ask to speak with someone in HR.

Which one of these works the best? It depends on the company.

Should you try all of them to see which works? Yes!

A word (or many words) of caution. The people you are contacting are generally busy. Usually they do recruiting on top of their regular jobs, which often means working overtime. They review résumés in their evenings and contact people by email then as well.

The point here is that these people are already working beyond their job expectations and I strongly suggest that you be very respectful of their time. Acknowledge that they are busy and ask if they have had time to review your application. Do not take much of their time. Thank them for it.

Taking those extra steps, if you are respectful, will significantly improve your chances of getting an interview (providing you have the technical qualifications, of course).

Effective emails

You need to send an email to a prospective employer. What is effective?

Subject: In the subject of the message include your name and the position to which you are applying, e.g., "Eric Derby, applicant for the Senior Talent Manager position." Most of the advice you will hear will be different from this: Sell! Make a pitch! Get their attention! The problem is that whatever it is that you do, odds are good that a lot of other people are trying to sell the same way. They might be selling software or a service or outsourcing. Unless you are in sales or marketing, where that might be expected, or unless you can find something this is truly unique, your best bet is to be direct. This is what has worked for me and has worked for my candidates.

Text: Keep it short and to the point. The longer the email is, the higher the probability that it will get closed and forgotten. Or put off until the recipient has free time, which would be never. The text should be at most three paragraphs, with at most two sentences per paragraph. This is not an absolute, but the shorter the better.

Topics: Try to keep to one or two topics or questions. I do the same thing myself when I am writing messages to my clients, whether in HR or hiring managers. If my messages are too long, I will often not get a response. If I have too many items or questions in an email, if I get a response, it will not answer all the questions.

Summary: keep messages short and to the point. Part of the reason is that you want to be respectful of the other person's time. Part is that you want to make it easy for the recipient to write a response.

Double check your spelling and grammar before you hit Send.

Personality tests

I do not know whether I have anything particularly good or bad to say about personality tests. Or as they are now called, behavioral assessments.

I know that what is typically used now is better than what was out years ago. The tests today are more focused on work-related attributes, those traits that will make a difference in the execution of the job.

The tests look for attributes and behaviors, and plenty of studies have been done to link those things to successfully working specific jobs.

In my experience, not that many companies use these tests. It generally costs a company for each test taken, so they tend to use them only where they think it is necessary.

I have one client that uses them only for leadership positions, whether technical or managerial. This client's interview process narrows down the candidates well, to those who probably will be successful. The client uses the personality test for confirmation that the company has selected the right person.

On two occasions I have asked clients that use these tests to allow me to take them and see the results. I found them to be accurate and in some cases insightful.

Always follow the instructions and answer questions honestly as asked. Many of the tests have built-in consistency checks, so that if you try to answer the questions they way that you think the company wants them answered and not honestly, the test will find the inconsistencies, and it will end in a rejection.

In a few cases, these tests might not be helpful. The first is when people who can do a job do not necessarily follow the traits typically associated with the position. If the company uses a good interview process, then the test to verify, this problem can be avoided. I have seen a company open a new interview discussion — an indication of some concern — with a candidate who was not the typical type for a position, about the position and the test results. The candidate was still hired and successful in the position.

Second, and a bigger problem, is when a company uses the test to knock people out rather than to just use it as a confirmation after a strong interview process. My experience is that this does not happen often. Companies have enough reasons to reject people without paying for a test to help them with this.

Finally, do not expect to see the results of the test unless you are hired. Most companies will not release results except to employees.

Freelance work

You do not want a full-time job working for someone else. You just want some work as needed and in effect want to be self-employed.

How do you go about that?

First, I would not suggest this unless you already have a reasonable amount of expertise or experience in your field. If you do not have any experience or reputation, this is going to be very difficult.

Next, realize that this is not going to be doing just the thing that you love to do. People that quit their day job so they can freelance and focus on the part they like best do not understand (yet) the nature of being self-employed.

You are now the accountant, sales and marketing person, legal department, computer technician, office manager and garbage collector. You will have more jobs than you had before and may have less time to focus on what you really want to do.

I am not saying this is a bad thing. I do this myself. I am just telling you what to expect. I know a guy whom I coached for weeks about starting his own software consulting company. After about half a year, he was tired of all the work he was doing that was not software development, especially the need to focus on sales. He got a job working for someone else and was much happier. It does not work for everyone.

You need to account for all the above things when determining your rate.

How do you get more freelance work?

Always be selling. No matter what you do, you need to always be selling yourself.

You need to be able to ask your satisfied clients for more work. You need to be able to ask your clients whom they know who might need your help. You need to be able to go to endless networking events (even if you are an introvert like myself) to constantly make new contacts.

The biggest item: inbound marketing. What this means is that you need to set yourself up as an expert in your field. You need to find places where you can help people for free. For example, I provide free workshops for the unemployed like "The Visual Résumé" and "Networking for Introverts." I have a blog for potential clients where I write about how to build a great staffing process.

Note that you are not giving away all your secrets. You are giving a free sample, enough to get them to want more. Give away too much, and they will not need you. You give enough that they know you are a Subject Matter Expert (SME) and will want to hire you if they have a project.

This generally means a lot of writing. Or maybe free events. Whatever it takes to get your name out there.

It may not be there

The job you want may not be there.

No matter how much you want it, or how hard you search, the job you want may not be there.

I know someone who was a machinist and was laid off along with thousands of others. There were not many other jobs for machinists in that city. The competition for those few jobs was fierce. Clearly not everyone found a new position in their field.

You may need to take a hard look at your skill set and the available jobs in the market to see whether you have a reasonable chance of finding the position you want.

I am not trying to kill your dreams of the perfect job, just insert a dose of realism. There may not be a demand for the work you do.

You do have options.
- You can move to another location where there are more jobs.
- You can get training to get into a new occupation.
- You can start your own company.

I am not saying that all these options will be available for everyone. You may have a sick parent and not be able to move. The point is that you may need to be flexible.

I believe that everyone can find work that they enjoy.

Be willing to fight for what you want and be open for new ways to make that happen.

CHAPTER TWELVE: Networking

Informational interviews

Ick. Informational interview? Most people cringe at the suggestion.

The term is terrible. People avoid them, and I think the biggest reasons are:
- it implies a level of formality that people do not like.
- people think the interviewer will try to pressure the interviewee into helping them get a position where the interviewee works.

My solution is to use a different name.
- Job Search Advice Meeting.
- Networking Meeting.

These are much less intimidating.

Most people like to give advice. They feel flattered if you ask for their advice. And while people are always busy, many more will meet with you if you politely ask for their help.

You *are* asking for help. You are asking for advice and opinions. It is a more honest and direct approach.

Yes, there are some people who may have to put aside their ego to ask for help, but as I have already said, a job search is hard work, and you should ask for help when you can.

What could you ask in the meeting?
- Do you have any suggestions for my career marketing plan? (Hint: send it in advance)
- Do you have any suggestions for my resumé? (Hint: send it in advance)
- What is it like working in this field?
- What will help me to be successful?
- Do you know of any jobs that I could apply for?
- Do you know any other people who could help me?
- What do you think are my strengths? Weaknesses?
- What are your favorite job search hints?

What should you avoid in the meeting? Asking for a job.

What else should you do?

- If you do not like or do not agree with the advice, keep it to yourself. This is a time to listen, not argue.
- Express appreciation for the person's time and advice.

Using these methods to meet with people will get you more meetings and speed up your job search.

Networking: still the best way

Jack was looking for a job. He sent an email to Jill to tell her he was looking and to ask whether she would meet for lunch. Jill said that a new position had just been approved in her company. The job had not even been posted yet. Jack sent Jill his résumé. Three weeks later Jack started his new job and took Jill out to lunch to say thank you.

Networking is still the best way to find a new job. It has been that way for a long time, and it will continue to be that way.

I am not saying that you should not use other methods for a job search. Use agencies. Use internet searches. Use job boards. Use all the other methods mentioned earlier.

Knowing people and connecting with people you know has the highest percentage of success. I have seen a range of numbers that show from 40 to 85 percent of jobs are found via networking. It is always higher than any other job search method.

The real key here is to stay connected with people. That can be a challenge all by itself.

It will not be a surprise that I will suggest staying connected with people on LinkedIn. Your profile belongs to you, so when you move to a new company, you will maintain your connections. You can build your network as you move to new jobs, and you can stay in touch with people as they move to new jobs. It is a very effective tool, and if you do not have a profile now, I suggest that you make one.

Join networking or professional groups. Do volunteer work.

Stay connected, and when you need your network, it will be there for you to tap into.

Under-used alumni

In my time as a recruiter, I have placed many people who attended RIT, my college. I met a lot of people there, people who became lifelong friends or peers.

I have used alumni groups to network. It is very effective for me.

I think that contacting college alumni may be the most under-used networking opportunity.

My friend John's wife had found a great job in Austin, Texas, so they were moving. John wanted my help finding a job there. I did not have any clients or recruiting allies in that city. I sent a message out to my alumni network about John, providing a quick overview of his skills. Several people got back to me about job opportunities. Several weeks later, John accepted a new position found through one of my contacts.

My suggestions:

- Call your college about local alumni events. Even if you do not live near your college, there may be events for alumni near you. This is a great way to connect with more people who went to your college.
- If you are working, and know of a job opening, send it to your local alumni representative. Or contact your company's HR to help them to connect with the Career Services group at your college for posting jobs.
- If you are looking for a job yourself, contact your college Career Services group to get set up for using its job search system. The office is always happy to help alumni.
- If you are a recent graduate, contact Alumni Services for the names of people who work at your target companies, or who live in your target location. The group may not be able to provide you with some information because it is confidential, but will find a way to help if asked.
- Most colleges also have LinkedIn and Facebook groups that you can join.

Networking events

You know I am an introvert.

I do not like going to networking events. They are exhausting.

I am a recruiter and a public figure. I need to do it. I need to connect to people and keep my name out there.

There are countless articles about how to "work" a networking event. Most of those neither "work" for me nor for many of the people I know. The key is that I have learned ways to go to these events that "work" for me.

These events are especially hard for introverts, but let me tell you a secret. Introverts can network too. Do not let the media tell you any different. When I run a "Networking for Introverts" workshop, people learn about ways that they like to network, and by the end it is hard to get people to be quiet.

Whatever your type, here are some things to try.

- Make a target for the number of new people you want to meet. I generally keep my goals small, like three. My goal is to enjoy an event, not just meet new people.
- Write something on your name tag that will get people's attention. "Ask me about how to build a runner bean teepee."
- Talk with people you know until you are comfortable. Stay at the event only as long as you are comfortable.
- Bring gifts or gimmicks, such as a handful of chocolate bars (with your business card attached), and let people know that you will give one out to each new person you have a conversation with. Word will get around, and people will come to you.
- My personal favorite is the buddy system. Either go to the event with a friend, or buddy-up with someone when you get there. The objective is for each of you to take turns introducing your buddy to someone else in the room. This is easier than just introducing yourself to a new person, because one of the two buddies already has a relationship with the new person. It takes off much of the pressure.
- Try to find new ways to make it fun that work for you.

Career fairs

A career fair can be a great opportunity. Or it can be dizzying. Here are some suggestions:

- Look at the list of companies attending before you go. Do some basic research on each company to see whether they have positions that might interest you. Do some extra research for any companies on your target list.
- Leave the backpack and coat in your car or at a coat check or another safe place. Have a professional folder or folio with copies of your résumé, your marketing plan, business cards and list of companies to talk with.
- If it is a large career fair, do not feel you must talk with each company there. Focus on talking with your target companies. If you have time for more than that, it is a bonus round.
- Dress your best. Go to the restroom and check your hair and clothes before you enter the fair.
- Asking what the company does is like screaming "I am unprepared!" to the room. If you do not know what the company does, ask for a flier and go read it, or look it up on your phone. Then go back and talk with the recruiter once you are informed.
- Have a short introduction ready. This should be similar to the objective in your résumé and cover three things: title, what is great about you and what you are going to do for them. It is a short and focused sales pitch.
- Be ready with a résumé, but also understand that many companies no longer collect résumés and want you to apply only online.
- If you are in a line, pay attention to whether the company is collecting résumés. Even if you hear that they are not, offer one anyway (after making your introduction). Sometimes if the person is impressed, they will take the résumé even if they are not generally taking them.

- If the recruiter takes your résumé and writes something on the back that is generally a good sign. Even if you see what they write I would suggest against trying to figure out what it means. Most recruiters have codes that they will use to determine what to do with the résumé when they get back to the office, and everyone uses something different. I will tell you my own codes, even though they will probably not be useful to you. If it is a good candidate and should be interviewed, I write a "+". If it is a very good candidate and should probably be hired, I write a "++". If I write a few letters it may be an abbreviation for the name of my client or might be the initials of the hiring manager.
- If they do not want a résumé, offer a business card.
- They may give you a card or paper with instructions to apply online. If they ask you to apply online, do it that night. Do not wait.
- Ask for the business card of a person with whom you should follow up. Do not expect to get a card. If you get one, it will probably be something generic. If you get a real business card, that means you have probably done well, and you could contact that person the day after the job fair ends.
- If you get a card and are also instructed to apply online, do that application that evening and then send an email to the contact telling the person that you have applied, and thanking them for their time.
- Whomever you meet in person at the company table, whether a recruiter or a hiring manager, express sincere appreciation for their time before leaving.

LinkedIn

John was recommended to me by another candidate whom I have worked with. I did the first thing that I generally do when I am told about a new person. I looked him up on LinkedIn. I did not see him. I tried variations on his name. No luck. I went to the employer page of the company where he was employed, and from there linked to the employees. Still nothing. The next day I received his résumé, and after talking with him I found that he did not have a LinkedIn profile. He had been in his position for many years and had never needed it.

It happens. On rare occasions I do find someone who does not yet have a LinkedIn profile.

What is much more common is to find people with profiles that have almost no information on them. Is this important? If you are looking for a job it is important. If you want people to find you for jobs that are relevant to you, then you need to have those details on your profile.

As a recruiter I use LinkedIn every day. I typically have multiple tabs open. I use it for searching for people. When I get a call from a new candidate, I will be looking up the profile as we start a conversation.

LinkedIn is not optional for most people. It is the biggest and most-used professional networking tool there is. Having a profile is important. Having a good profile is more important. Keeping your profile up to date is important.

Considering that it is constantly changing I am not going to go into too much detail. I will provide some general guidelines for creating a good profile. My recommendation is to find one of the well-known people who regularly write about LinkedIn and follow that person. That will keep you up to date as the tool changes.

I finally got my foot in the door at Company Z and was working with their recruiter, Sam. I really liked him. He was smart and enthusiastic and responded to calls or emails quickly. He understood the details of the positions that he was recruiting for. I was really looking forward to working with him and getting to know him. Then one day I called, and he was gone. What also disappointed me was that I had not connected with him on LinkedIn. I did not know what happened or where he had gone. Many years later I found him working as a recruiting manager in a large NYC technical company. It was nice to reconnect with him, but I felt not staying connected was a lost opportunity.

For most people this is the best value from LinkedIn. Connecting with people and staying connected. Build your network. Connect with people whom you are working with now. Go to companies you have worked for in the past and reconnect with the people there. The ability to connect with people and stay connected with them is the greatest value this tool provides.

LinkedIn profile

Here's an overview of the most important aspects of your LinkedIn profile.

Headline: Make sure this is your current title. A little creativity is fine, and can get you more attention, providing people can understand your primary job title. If you are not employed, it should say that you are looking for work and should also include the title of the job that you are looking for.

Some recruiters disagree with posting that you are unemployed. They say it makes it look like you are desperate for a job. I think it makes you honest and upfront. As a recruiter, if I see a headline that says the person is looking for a job, I will immediately open that person's profile in a new tab, so that I will look at it that day. A person who is not employed does not need a two-week notice and can start a new position more quickly, which is a benefit. Also, I have been unemployed myself. If I can help a person who is unemployed I will.

About: This is your summary. The first two to three lines are the most important, because that is what people will initially see if they look at your profile. These lines should be catchy and include a summary of your accomplishments. The format of the rest should be different from your résumé, but it should include much of the same information. It should include your skills sets and an overview of your work experience. It can also include something about your passions and interests. Make sure it is well-written without getting too long.

Picture: I prefer that people have a good professional picture with their profile. If I am going to meet with someone whom I have not seen before, it is helpful. The main reason some suggest against a picture is to avoid discrimination. Considering that a very high percentage of people have pictures in their profile, not having one often seems odd now, which can be more of a negative.

Work experience: Put in something about each of the positions you have worked. One of the ways that people can find you is by the companies that you have listed, so including all employers is helpful. You do not need to add in all the details of each position. A quick overview of skills used and primary accomplishments is generally plenty of detail. If they want more detail, they can look at your résumé or ask you in for an interview.

Recommendations: This is one of my favorite parts, but is not used as much as it could be. When LinkedIn first started to get popular, recommendations were important. The goal was to have five. To get that many, you often had to give more than that first. As a recruiter, if I am interested in a candidate, I will very often look at the recommendations. These can tell me a lot about a person in just a few minutes. It is worth your time to get good recommendations.

CHAPTER THIRTEEN: Working with a Third-party Recruiter

Definitions

For purposes of this book I am dividing this into two groups: agencies and headhunters. This chapter does not include any discussion of internal or corporate recruiters.

Agency: Staffing agency, staffing firm, temporary agency, employment service, and placement firm, etc. Typically, these are companies that are large enough that the functional aspects of the company have been split into different positions.

Headhunter: Professional recruiter, independent recruiter, headhunter, executive recruiter, and technical recruiter, etc. Typically, these are small companies or sometimes only one person.

The term headhunter is not always liked or appreciated. Some people think the term has derogatory connotations. Others like it because people understand what the term is, even if it is not accurate. I suggest asking a recruiter for their preferred title before using this term.

These definitions are not set in stone. There may be an Executive Search Firm that has several Executive Recruiters and is large enough to have an office staff. Many combinations are possible. I am an unusual case myself because I work both as an external technical recruiter and perform onsite recruiting for some of my clients.

Agency methods

How do staffing agencies really work?

First, they have account managers (or people with some similar title) whose job it is to find clients who need staffing help and get a contract signed with them. They get the details of the positions and pass those on to the recruiters (via whatever agency software or ATS package they use). The account manager is generally the single point of contact with their client. All client activity is logged in the computer.

Recruiters have the job of finding candidates to fit the jobs that the account managers bring in. They generally have a database of candidates that they can search, which has previous résumés and contact information and contact history. The recruiters do job postings and interviews and send the viable candidates to the account manager to send to the client.

Office staff take care of the hiring paperwork and the office's day-to-day functions.

There is generally a person who runs the office. The title is generally something like director, since account manager and office manager titles are taken, and it needs to sound more important. This is the person who manages the recruiters and account managers and who is responsible for reporting to corporate if the office is part of a larger agency.

The director's job is to drive the metrics. In an agency everything is a numbers game. A certain percentage of calls lead to a percentage of interviews. Interviews lead to submittals (also called send-outs), which lead to on-site interviews, which lead to offers. At each stage, the numbers get smaller, so the key is to have enough people in every stage of the process. The job of the director is to track this and motivate people to keep up to volume. The name of the game is quantity, not quality.

Enough quantity at the start of the process will generally provide enough placements to hit the financial goals of the office.

Agency recruiters

Agency recruiters have a hard job and often get a bad reputation.

To keep up the pipeline, they need to make a high number of calls or emails to candidates every day. A typical goal might be 50. Then they need to be doing interviews each day, whether in person or on the phone. They need to qualify the candidate (or disqualify, as the case may be) and move on to the next candidate. They need to hit their numbers.

This works for some people better than others. I know recruiters who can make a call, get key questions answered and be off the phone in 10 minutes.

That did not work for me. I liked to get into longer conversations with my candidates to build a better rapport and relationship. That did not work for an agency that I worked for several years ago.

I was on a call with a candidate. I thought the call was going well and I was building a good rapport with the candidate. After 15 minutes I saw the director giving me funny looks from his fishbowl (where he had a computer that could tell him how long I had been on the phone). After 30 minutes he was standing behind me tapping his foot.

The point here is that agency recruiters are expected to hit numbers. Some might like to chat longer and get to know you better, but that is not what is expected in the agency. They are paid to hit the numbers and make placements. If they do not do that, they will not be working for the agency very long.

I would also like to mention that agency recruiters do not rake in money. With every placement the office generally gets the largest cut, and the remainder is split by the account manager (who brought in the job) and the recruiter (who brought in the candidate).

The biggest financial winner is the agency or office, not the recruiter.

Understand that recruiters who work for most agencies have quotas to fill for the number of people they talk with, number of new calls they make, number of résumés submitted, etc. They probably want to help more and spend more time talking with you, but they are under a lot of pressure.

How to find an agency

Years ago, I had a person whom I had placed who was moving to another state. He asked for my help. I went to work trying to find a small agency in the target city in that state, someone that had a similar style and work ethic to my own. It was difficult. Given the size of the city it should not have been all that hard. I kept finding big agencies. Most of the smaller agencies I found were rude to me. I did not even want a cut of the placement fee. I had placed this person into his job and to get paid to help him leave was not ethical (even if it was because his wife was being transferred).

Finding a staffing agency is easy now. Even small agencies have their own website. A simple internet search including your target location will provide you with pages of them. In addition, you can call friends to ask for referrals. You can contact your local alumni association to see whether there are local alumni who have suggestions.

The harder part is finding the right kind of agency for your search.

The first thing to consider is the field of expertise. You want to be working with an agency that understands what you do.

Next think about whether direct placement or contract positions are in your career marketing plan. Some agencies will do both, some just direct placement, some just contractor placement.

The next thing to consider is the size of your target companies. Quite a few agencies work only with the largest employers. You do not need an agency that works with all the companies in your target list but note what size companies they typically work with.

Thinking about these things that you want, look at the agencies from your search and do some research. Look at their websites to see what type of work they do. Sometimes agencies list their clients on their site.

When you have narrowed it down to a few companies, call them. Ask all the same questions you just researched. Odds are good that if they have a recruiter who knows what you do, you will have been connected directly with that person. While you are talking with them on the phone, do the same thing that recruiters do: Look them up on LinkedIn. Review their profile as you are talking with them. (This is such a cool reversal; more people need to do this.)

If you are not sure, you can ask for references. Call the references and ask them the same questions.

If you are not comfortable with the agency, do not send them your résumé.

Not all agencies are created equal. This is an industry that can be cutthroat and unethical. Fortunately, most agencies treat people well and have high ethical standards. Some will take more time to help people even if there is no direct payoff. Find an agency or two that fit into your overall job search strategy and build those relationships.

How to work with a third-party recruiter

- Know what you want.
- Know whether you are looking for a contract or a direct placement. Some companies do both; some do

CHAPTER THIRTEEN: Working with a Third-party Recruiter

only contractors; some (like me) do only direct placement.
- Know what you want in company size, culture and vertical market.
- In case you had not noticed, these items are all things that should be in your career marketing plan.
- Ask up front whether they place people in your profession. You can ask how many people they place, but the recruiter may not be allowed to share that information.
- Do not use the agency as your only method of job search. It should be one of many methods. If you are reasonably happy with your position and looking for something better, and not in a hurry, then you might be able to use a good recruiter as your sole source.
- Make sure you know where they are sending your résumé and that they will not send it to a client without your permission.
- Keep track of all job applications you have made, whether through agencies, at job fairs, online, etc., so that you can prevent duplicate résumé presentations and even discussions.
- Ask if they want to see your career marketing plan. This can help the recruiter know what you are looking for. But understand that an agency recruiter may not have time to look at your plan.
- If the agency does not have any work that fits you, they may not get back to you quickly.
- If the recruiter has sent your résumé to a client, they may not get back to you if they have not heard back from the client.
- Understand that while a recruiter makes money by placing you in a new position, it is their client that pays the bills. The client's opinion trumps your opinion.
- If you are treated with disrespect, leave and find another firm. There are plenty more.

Pros of working with a third-party recruiter

- It will not cost you anything.
- They may know of openings that you would not find elsewhere. Agencies try very hard to get and keep exclusive clients.
- They generally have direct contact with hiring managers. This means that if they are interested in you, your résumé will go directly to that hiring manager.
- They can quickly tell you your market value and what the market might pay, depending on your skills, experience, company size and other factors.
- They can sometimes get you more feedback from an interview than you would have gotten on your own.
- They may have a wealth of information about their client. If they have been working with the client for a while, they may have a good knowledge of the culture and work environment. You can work with them to determine whether you would be a good fit.
- They have a good knowledge of the strength of their part of the market, including economics, history and expected future.
- They may be able to provide some coaching on various aspects of the job search.
- They have experience negotiating job offers.

Cons of working with a third-party recruiter

- If you are not a fit for any of their jobs, they will not get back to you quickly, sometimes not at all.
- They are generally busy and can be hard to reach, and when you reach them, they have limited time for you.
- They place a relatively small percentage of the people they talk with and represent. I heard one agency say that they placed 40 percent of the people they interviewed. But most are a much smaller percentage, generally less than 10 percent, some even less than 5 percent.

- They may not really understand your expertise, and could present you wrong, or set you up for an interview for the wrong type of job.
- They may not have as good a relationship with their client as they lead you to believe.
- They probably cannot help you if you are looking to change careers.
- They may have limited time available to help you with your résumé or other coaching.

Agencies and résumés

Historically agencies wanted your résumé in Microsoft Word format. This was because:
- They could easily edit the résumé to take off your contact information. This would force the client to work through them to set up interviews and reduce the possibility that the client would try to go around the agency.
- They could easily add their own stamp to the résumé, with the agency name and contact information, to provide a clear trail of the source of the candidate.
- Some agencies would edit your résumé to put it into their own format. I do not see this much anymore.
- Clients would almost always have Microsoft Word, so it was a safe format to use.

Most agencies now have software that allows them to edit PDF files, including adding an origin stamp and taking off the contact information. As a result, you can now send PDF files.

If you use open source tools, Google Docs or other formats, I suggest you save the file to Word or PDF format before sending it. Many recruiters can open these other formats, but using the most common tools ensures this and makes it easier on the recruiter. Make sure that you view the file after you convert to make sure that the format was not changed or damaged in the conversion.

Occasionally a recruiter will make suggestions to you for your résumé. Most often this will happen if you are a candidate they can place, but your résumé could use some improvement. If you have a better résumé, then they have a better chance at placing you. Often the recruiter will know what their client likes to see on a résumé.

If the recruiter gives you a referral to a résumé writer, it probably means that you have potential, but that the recruiter does not have the time to help you with extensive résumé changes. It is a nice way to say that your résumé needs help.

Headhunters

A headhunter is different from a staffing agency. The headhunter typically is hired by their client to find people for specific direct-hire positions. They often work at pulling people out of companies that compete with their client to get the best skills fit. They look to take the best people away from the competition and place them with their client.

True headhunters are not all that common today. They were more common in the days when people would work at a job and intend to stay there indefinitely. Today people are more open to changing jobs and keeping their eyes open for new opportunities. They are more likely to be proactive in their job search.

It has become harder for a headhunter to do their traditional work. If a headhunter does find someone who was not looking and interests that person in a new position with their client, then it is also likely that the candidate will start looking for other positions on their own.

Often I see headhunters as specialists in a narrowly defined field. For example, I was working on-site for a food manufacturing client doing recruiting. During my time there I was surprised at the number of recruiters who specialized in the food and beverage industries (I know this, because more and more kept calling me).

A recruiter with this type of specialization would build up their network of people in the field over the course of many years. Then when they were working with a client, they would look through their candidates for people who might fit.

How do you find one?

Use the same methods that you would use to look for a staffing agency, except focus more on the area of expertise and less on location. Some may have a presence with companies in your area, even if they are located across the country.

If they do not fit what you are looking for, ask whom they know that might fit. Recruiters often know others in similar fields.

CHAPTER THIRTEEN: Working with a Third-party Recruiter

Placement agent

Also called a career management company.

In the past it was possible to find people who would work directly for the candidate, including getting paid by the candidate, and actively work to help them find their next position.

This is not the same as a coach. This person would be your own agent.

These people would actively call companies on your behalf. They typically have a high number of clients they have worked with and have strong industry contacts. Their clients like to work with them, because they bring forward strong vetted candidates with no fee attached.

Like a coach, they will help you with your résumé, help you hone interview skills and assist you will all phases of the search process. You pay them to find you the right job.

Their fee model is the opposite of an agency or headhunter. They charge a fee to the candidate and not to their client companies.

These companies are not cheap. Fifteen years ago, they cost $3,000, and they would work only with candidates they felt they could successfully place, but they also gave no guarantee. I did some quick searches today, and claims of scams about these companies abound, including the one that I knew. I do not recommend this as a good option.

Candidate control

If you have not worked in the staffing industry, you may not have heard the term "candidate control."

The idea here is that the agency wants to control all aspects of the hiring process to make sure that nothing would go wrong. All the steps are plotted and planned.

This is what I was taught when I started as a recruiter. I am not sure how this started, but I could guess the reasons would be

- that competition in the industry has often been fierce and there is a desire for perfection.
- that on occasion a candidate would do something that would cause them to be knocked out of the process, thus costing the agency a commission.

My problem with this is that it dehumanizes the entire process. It treats each candidate like a number. It shows lack of trust in the candidate.

I do not pretend to control the process. I like my stomach to be ulcer-free.

I prefer to get to know the candidate and their goals. If I spend enough time talking with the candidate, I will know whether the person is a fit for my client in terms of both culture and skills. I will know the needs of my candidate and will know whether the person needs a different work schedule or something that might not be expected.

I know how to coach my candidates. I do my best to help a candidate be prepared for an interview. It does not always work. I had a candidate for a position that I knew he could perform quite well. But he was nervous and talked too much and too fast at the first interview. The employer considered this (at my suggestion) and allowed for a second interview. I coached the candidates to slow down and listen more. He was still too nervous, because he had a family to support, and did not slow down. He did not get the job.

We all do the best we can. My job is to screen the candidates, sell them on the company if it is a fit, and coach them as needed. My job is to find the right person for the job.

Your job is to be the best you can be and find work that is best for you. You don't need to be controlled for that to happen.

It is fortunate that this type of behavior is no longer typical in agencies.

CHAPTER FOURTEEN: Interview Preparation

Interview overview

First, let's not pretend that interviewing is easy, at least for most people.

I give presentations on my recruiting services to potential clients all the time. I have done it so many times that I am quite comfortable and relaxed.

Yet on the rare occasions that I go on an interview I still get quite nervous. One time my knees were shaking and I was happy that a table hid that.

Here is a quick overview of what you can do to perform better during the interview:

- Reread the job description. Bring a copy with you to review while you are waiting.
- Practice. Find some friends to do practice interviews with you. It may sound silly and it may feel fake, but the practice will make you a lot more comfortable when it comes time for the real interview.
- Research the company and the interview team. Ask your network for reviews about the company culture. The more you know about the company and its people, the more relaxed you are likely to be in the interview.
- Learn a simple relaxation technique that is not noticeable. The one I use most: Sit up straight with your face forward. Keeping your face still, move your eyes upward in a 12 o'clock direction, but not so far that it becomes uncomfortable. Focus your eyes on something. Hold your eyes in that position. Over the next minute or two, you will notice that your heart rate and breathing will start to slow down. You can do this while waiting in the lobby or between interviews.
- Bring a list of questions about the job and company. Asking questions will get the pressure off you and give you time to think and relax.

Your résumé got you in the door; now the interview(s) will determine a possible offer.

Interview process

There are no standards for the interview process.

What can you expect? Over the course of your search, you can expect a wide variety:

- Time of day: There is no typical time you can set that is more likely to get you an offer. There may be differences within the company, but no standard answer. As a candidate you should know whether you interview better in the morning or afternoon. If you are given options, you can get an interview time that fits you. If the interview team is very busy, you may not have much of a choice.
- Group vs. individual interviews: Some companies will have each person interview you individually. Others will set up two at a time to interview you to reduce the amount of time you spend on-site. Some companies will do group interviews. The primary theory behind this is that everyone will hear the answer to the questions, so you will not be asked the same question many times. Group interviews tend to be more stressful.
- If you are in a group interview, it can help to know who the actual hiring manager is. If you know who this person is, it is especially important to answer questions from him (or her) in a quality fashion.
- Duration of interview: An initial interview by a manager could be as short as 30 minutes. An interview for a VP of engineering could be six hours, including a lunch.
- Rounds of interviews: Some companies will have one interview that is two hours long and will decide immediately. Some companies will have as many as five different interviews over the course of several weeks. Sometimes this depends on the size of the company. Larger companies will often have more interviews, but that is not always that case. I know

CHAPTER FOURTEEN: Interview Preparation

one small company that will do three to five interviews, depending on the position.
- Initial interviews: Sometimes a manager will do the first interview with a candidate, and if that works, will bring the candidate back to interview with the rest of the team. This reduces the impact of time spent interviewing by the team.
- Rounds of interviews may also be dependent on the possible interaction of the position with other teams. The more a position calls for interaction with members of other teams, the more likely there will be more interviews, and more interviewers.
- The hardest part about multiple interviews is that you need to succeed many times to get the job. One failure can get you knocked out.

If you do not know what the process is and the company does not mention it, then ask.

Interview schedule

When you are invited in for an in-person interview with a company, ask for an interview schedule. Some companies provide these; many do not. Some of those that do not will give you the schedule if you ask.

The schedule provides you with information that can help you prepare for the interview:
- The duration of each portion of the interview.
- The total expected length of the interview.
- The names of the people you will be speaking with, so you can research them.
- The number of people in each interview portion (i.e. will it be one-on-one or two-on-one, etc.).
- Knowing the schedule can help you be more comfortable and less nervous.

If the interview goes through lunchtime, and there is no lunch scheduled, you can ask for a lunch break to be provided. A hungry interviewee will not likely be at their best, so it is better for all involved to have a lunch break. It is a very reasonable request.

If you get the names of the people on an interview schedule, doing some research on each of them can be helpful, if nothing more than looking up their profiles on LinkedIn. If you know the job function of each interviewer you can know what types of questions to expect from each.

If you are working with an external recruiter, that person might be able to provide you with additional information about the people you are interviewing with. You could get hints about things to say or not say. For example, one of my clients had a lot of hockey fans on its staff, so talking about hockey was a great way to, uh, break the ice.

What if they will not give you a schedule? At that point there is not much you can do. If they would not give you a schedule, you could decline the interview, but that would not help. Work with what you have. Take notes, especially the names and titles of the people you are speaking with.

Researching the job and company

How much should you know about the company before the first interview? Is just reading its website enough? The job description sounded great, and you applied for the job. They called you in for an interview, but how do you know that you really want to work for that company?

Research: You need to look at quite a few places to get a good idea of what the company is like. It is worth your time. It could mean years of your life in misery or happiness.

- Company website. Look at more than just the products. Look to see whether they have client testimonials. Look for press releases. Look to see if they have employee testimonials. Are they socially responsible?
- Search local newspapers for stories about the company. You will find some with an internet search. You might need to go to the library. Check out their social media platforms. If it is a public company, look at the stock performance.
- Look for people you know who work there. Take them out to lunch and ask about the work environment. Look for people you know who formerly worked there. They might give you a different perspective.

- Glassdoor.com: I am a bit wary of recommending this site, because it started as a complaint site where people would rant about companies they once worked for. Much of what you read will be negative, and from people who were unhappy to be employed there, but this does not mean that the company is a bad place to work. Look for patterns. These can lead to good questions to ask in an interview. For example: A client of mine had a number of complaints that the work changed frequently and without much notice. That was true. When the company's clients called and wanted production lines changed, it had to be done, and done quickly. This is not necessarily bad. If you are a person who likes variety and change and a fast pace, it would be good. If you are a person who likes consistency and a regular pace, it would be bad.

When you are done, you should have a good understanding of the company and know that it is a place where you would want to work, even before the interview. Your research should supply you with more questions about the company.

Interview your manager

One of the hardest parts of the interview is interviewing the person who might be your future manager. It can be difficult asking this person questions, but it is important. One of the most common reasons people leave their jobs is because of their manager. You need to make sure, at the interview, that you can work well with this person.

Ask questions:
- What is your management style?
- What is your conflict management style?
- How much do you interact with your team?
- Why did you come to work for this company?
- What do you like about working here?
- How has this group performed recently?
- Are any changes planned in the next year?

- How is the company performing this year?
- What long range plans do you have for this group?
- Are there any negatives about working in this group or for this company?

This is your time to ask questions. If you want to be comfortable with your job, you need to be comfortable with your boss.

Talk with a peer

When you look at the interview schedule and review the interviewers, look to see if one of the people you will be speaking with is working in a similar position. If you do not see part of the interview process that is a one-on-one with a peer, then ask for that.

A lot of information can be gained from this portion of the interview, and it is worth your time to ask for a peer interview. When you talk with that person, you can ask about the day-to-day work life.

Remember that the interview is a two-way process. You need to use the interview to learn about the job and the company. Here are some of the questions you can ask a peer:

- What is the management style of the boss?
- Does the company actively work to take care of employees?
- Does the company try to pay market wages?
- How do the benefits compare?
- Does management listen to employee suggestions?
- How would you describe the culture?

The point of these questions is to get a better and more accurate picture of the company and the job. You can get a better idea if you will be happy working for this company. Management and HR tend to paint a pretty picture of the company and the job. While you hope their perspectives will be accurate, you can learn more from a peer interview.

If you do not have a peer interview as part of your interview process and if you know that the company is interested in you, then you can ask for a peer interview. If that company asks why, you can tell them the truth — that you want to learn more about the company culture from a person with whom you would be working.

Dress code

How should you dress for an interview?

The simple answer: the best "business formal" attire you have.

On rare occasions you will be told, during an interview, that you did not need to dress so well. If that occurs, no one will count it against you that you overdressed.

However, if you dress poorly for an interview, it can, and most often will, be counted against you.

The exceptions to this:
- If someone from the company tells you how to dress, or more specifically tells you that you do not need to dress "business formal" or the like.
- If you are working with an external recruiter, and that person tells you how to dress.

To summarize, it is better to be more formal than too casual.

You may also notice that all my statements on this page are gender-neutral. The need for gender-specific clothing for an interview (or for that matter for a job) is fading.

Tattoos and piercings

A tough and controversial subject.

I will be blunt and upfront. It is legal for a company not to hire you because of piercings and/or tattoos. These are not protected rights. You can choose to have piercings and tattoos that cannot be covered but you are doing that as a choice, and the company can choose not to hire you if they feel that they are inappropriate or offensive, either in the workplace or with respect to customer relations.

There is a lot more openness toward these now, but still many people dislike them. For the purposes of most interviews I suggest taking out piercings that can be removed and covering tattoos that can be covered. While at the interview, ask the HR representative or the hiring manager about the company policy.

Observing the company during the interview or as you are given a tour is also important. Make note of people with piercings or tattoos that show. This could give you some idea of what the company policy is. It may also be obvious with retail or restaurant jobs.

A job you like and the way that you like to express body art may be different, and that is OK. You can be happy with both at different times.

Common questions asked

I am listing here many of the most asked interview questions that are not specifically related to the job. Make sure you review the common questions (and possibly hundreds more on the internet if you are especially enthusiastic) and have answers for them.

- What interests you about our company? What do you like about our company?
- What interests you about this position? Why do you want this job?
- Why are you looking for a new position?
- What is your greatest professional achievement? (I wish more people would ask this one.)
- Tell me about yourself. (I wish people would not ask this one. Too open-ended.)
- Why should we hire you?
- What is your greatest strength?
- What is your greatest weakness?
- Why do you want to leave (or have left) your current job?
- How do you handle stress and pressure?
- Describe a difficult work situation and how you overcame it.
- Where do you see yourself in five years? (If you like what you are doing and want to keep doing that, just show that you also want to keep improving.)
- Where do you see yourself in 10 years? (If you want to do something different, but in your field, that can show growth, the company will not need to replace you in a few years.)

Most work-related questions will come in a STAR format, or if not, are questions that you can answer in this format. STAR = Situation, Task, Action, Result. Go through every job you worked and make sure you have some examples that fall into this format.

- Situation: Describe the problem.
- Task: Describe your assignment.

- Action: Describe the steps you took,
- Results: Describe the outcome of your actions.

Many of your examples will also fall into Storytelling (covered in another topic).

Questions that everyone hates

Strange questions. The first thing to understand about strange questions is that it is (most often) not the answers to questions that are important. Quite often the questions are there to test how you respond.

They want to see how you react to the questions. They want to see how you work: how you process the questions, how you come up with answers. Regardless of your answers, the way that you respond under stress in an interview is likely to be the same way that you would react under stress on the job.

I am not saying that I agree with strange questions. I think all the underlying information that is learned from asking those strange questions can also be learned from asking work-related questions.

I do not think that my opinion about this will change the world. Just do the best you can. If you want to prepare, you can go on-line and search for lists of strange interview questions. Have a friend test you on those before a real interview.

Trick questions. Some interviewers like trick questions. They make some interviewers feel they are smarter than the person they are interviewing. Some interviewers think that helps them find smart or creative people. The bottom line is that trick questions do not predict performance, so there is no real reason to ask them in an interview. You may encounter someone who likes trick questions. If you do, think about the long-term implications. Would you want to work for a person who tries to trip you up during an interview? What would working for that person be like every day? Do the best you can in the interview, but be wary before accepting an offer.

Illegal questions. In the U.S. it is illegal to ask questions about the following topics:
- Race, color or national origin
- Sex, gender identity or sexual orientation
- Pregnancy status
- Religion
- Disability

- Age or genetic information
- Citizenship
- Marital status or number of children

That said, sometimes these questions come up in an interview. Sometimes the interviewer has not been properly trained. Sometimes there is active discrimination. Sometimes the conversation gets very casual and the interviewer asks a question without thinking.

What do you do in this situation? You have options.

- Answer the question. If you think the question was asked innocently, you can answer the question, if you feel comfortable doing so. You are not required to do this.
- Answer the intent of the question. In many cases the question is really about your ability to do the job. You can respond in a way that tells the person that you are capable of doing the job without ever answering the discriminatory aspect.
- Question the question. You can ask how the question relates to your ability to perform the job. This may get the person to rethink their question, or possibly withdraw the question. Or it might cause a clarification, e.g., some jobs require handling of government security information, so there is a requirement that the candidate must be a U.S. citizen.
- Refuse to answer the question. You can politely tell the interviewer that the question is illegal and that you decline to answer it. This can cause a little more disruption to the interview than the options above.

It is important to know your rights and how to respond if you get a question on one of these topics.

Storytelling

"Do not give one-word answers to questions."

What do you say? If you have not been able to build rapport with the interviewer and have not gotten the interview to a conversational mode, a story is often the best way to answer a question.

Storytelling is the oldest method of teaching. By providing an example of what you have done, you are telling the interviewer a lot more than what the person asked. You are demonstrating your communication style. You are giving an example of how you solve a problem or how you work with a team.

What makes a good story?

A good story is one that is about a minute long, maybe up to two minutes, or maybe three for something especially important or complicated. It is better to err on the side of brevity than length. The story provides an example of something that you have accomplished, related to the question.

It can be an easy way to answer a question when you are nervous or stressed.

How do you make this work? Make a list of accomplishments that you have from various jobs. Go through your résumé. Go through old performance reviews. Ask friends and previous co-workers what they remember that you accomplished. Make a long list. (A funny example: I recently interviewed a candidate whom I knew from my first job after college. He remembered that I ran the company picnic 30 year ago. That is a good example of organization skills and delegation for me.)

Look at the list of the most common interview questions and play the matching game. Match your accomplishments with the most common questions.

Here is the real key.

Practice. Practice. Practice.

If you want to be able to tell your stories well, when under stress, you need to rehearse the stories.

Pay attention. Storytelling does not work with every interviewer. If you are getting negative reactions from your stories, stop the storytelling and try a different approach.

Standing out from the crowd

How do you differentiate yourself from all the other candidates who apply for the same position?

A good number of factors are going to be job- and company-dependent, but some of the ways that might help.

- Focus on what you can do for the company. The reason the job is open is because work needs to be done. Concentrate on showing them that you can do the job and do it well. Speak to your strengths.
- Show a history of rapid success. Have examples ready of how you have solved problems like the problems they have (see Topic on Storytelling).
- Allow your passion to show. Show your interest and enthusiasm about the work. Talk about why you find the job and company interesting. Talk about the things you hope to accomplish. Companies tend to hire people who want the job.
- Show how your skills match the job description. Get out a copy of it and talk about how you can do each of the tasks listed.
- Discuss your strengths. Show how your strengths will help the company and help you to do the job in a way that exceeds expectations.
- Be ready with examples of adaptability. Show how you have adapted to change. Demonstrate that you have quickly learned new skills on the job.
- Reference the achievements listed on your résumé. (If you do not have enough achievements there, you need to go back and revisit the résumé.)

CHAPTER FIFTEEN: The Interview

Everything is important

Everything is important in an interview, starting from the time you enter the company property. Here is a list of things to consider:

- Plan to arrive early.
- Some people drive the route the night before to make sure they know the way.
- If you have a smartphone, use the driving app to make sure that you know where you are going. This has helped me recently when I was going to meet a new client and thought I knew where to go but I was going to the wrong office complex.
- If you drive, park legally, even if it is a farther walk to the door.
- Ditch the chewing gum before you leave your car.
- Be presentable. Dress well, check your attire before you approach the front door.
- Open doors for others, regardless of your gender or their gender.
- Be polite and professional to everyone you meet, including the receptionist, housecleaning or the person watering the plants.
- If you are not familiar with the rules for a standard handshake learn them. Practice.
- Make eye contact.
- Sit up straight.
- Pay attention. When I go to visit potential new clients, I pay attention to the workplace while I am getting a tour. Are people laughing? Pulling out their hair? Smiling? Frowning? Having Nerf wars? Observe. You do not say anything about it but pay attention to the look and feel of the place.
- Also pay attention to the interviewers. Ask yourself the same questions as above. Pay attention to how

they treat you. Are you treated with respect? Like a number or a chore? Are they stressed or relaxed?
- Ignore the competition. Concentrate on being the best you can be. Concern about the competition will not improve your ability to interview (unless you are a highly competitive type, then maybe).
- Be polite and professional to everyone you meet (did I already say that? Well, it bears repeating).

I have heard stories of people getting jobs because of small positive things they did during an interview, and that people have been rejected because of small negative things.

Be yourself

"Just be yourself, and everything will be great."

No.

Be your best professional self.

You may have a great cosplay of Harley Quinn, but an interview is not the best time to show that.

Like a gem, every person has different facets or sides. The person you show to your family is not the same person you show to your friends and is not the same person you show to your partner.

Most people do not show the same side to their boss as to their co-workers.

When you go to an interview, present your best professional side, whatever that is for your career. An engineer will have a different presentation than a barista.

You do not need to be accepted for all your facets by your employer. You just need to show the part of you that can do the job well.

First 10 seconds

You have probably heard it said that the first 10 seconds of the interview sets the tone for the entire interview. This is true if you believe it to be true.

A poor start to an interview can be overcome.

I have been part of review teams where one interviewer stated that the interview started poorly, but that it had improved by the end. It is possible. Other than preparing better before the interview, what can you do?

Do not give up. Persevere. Keep trying.

If you were on the job and you made a mistake what would you do? Would you let it ruin your day? Or would you fix the problem? Odds are good that you would not let it bother you and correct it. Same thing in the interview. Acknowledge the problem to yourself and to the interviewer if needed. Apologize if needed. Then move on, presenting your best self. If you let the problem take over, you will not respond well in the rest of the interview and will have lost your shot at the job.

The best success stories are where something started poorly, or failed, but the person continued trying and overcame the obstacle. If you persevere and get past the problem, the interviewer may be more impressed, as you have just shown your ability to overcome adversity.

Parents

I was working on-site with a client, and the receptionist came to me with a problem. A candidate had brought his mother with him to the interview. Upon further examination, it turned out that the candidate spoke mainly Spanish. His mother wanted to come along as a translator. The problem was that his mother would not be able to be with him on the job. He needed to interview for the position based on his own capabilities. He was not allowed to have his mother with him during the interview.

You succeed or fail on your own. No one else can come to the interview with you.

While this may seem to be an extreme example, I have heard of other examples of parents coming along on an interview. It is best not to bring along friends or family. If you need them for transportation, have them drop you off at the interview site. Have the person go to a coffee shop or go shopping and wait for you to call after the interview.

Phone

In the middle of the interview, Bob pulled out his phone and started typing into it while Joe, the hiring manager, was talking. Joe thought that it was rude behavior and was about to mentally reject the candidate. Bob, however, added something relevant to the conversation while showing Joe his phone.

Could have been a disaster. Bob could have been rejected right there.

Mobile phones should be turned off before the interview, probably before you even enter the building. If you have a reason that your phone needs to be on, please explain that to the interviewer.

- I once interviewed a person whose wife was going in for surgery, and he needed to be available. He asked if he could leave his phone on. That he was even at the interview said to me that he was very interested in the position, and I had no problem with his phone being on.
- If you want to look something up on your phone during the interview it is generally best to ask and explain what you want to look up.

Otherwise it can come across as rude or that you are not interested in the position.

Keep the phone turned off.

On a related note, I also think it is rude if the interviewer keeps checking their phone every few minutes during the interview. I find it distracting and inconsiderate.

BYOD?

If you think the interview will be long enough that you will want a drink, it may be best to bring your own.

I was in a meeting with a new client. They offered me a drink and I asked for tea. While they were talking, I leaned back a little, the chair tilted much easier than I expected, and I spilled tea on my nice white shirt.

My solution: a non-spill professional cup. Not an open mug. Not something disposable from a coffee shop. Something professional and reusable.

Or a water bottle will do just fine.

This also solves another problem. Sometimes the company will offer you a drink. Sometimes they will not. If you bring your own, you will know you have a drink, and what you like. And reduce the odds of being embarrassed by spilling it on your clothes.

Bad interviewer

Sometimes the interviewer has no idea what they are doing. The person had not prepared, and clearly not had any training about how to do an interview. No plan. No objectives.

What do you do?

Take the lead. Run the interview.

You have been through interviews before. You know how they go. Think about the job the interviewer has and how that would relate to the job that you would be doing. Address your ability to do the job from their perspective. If you were talking with an engineer you talk about your engineering skills, and how they would relate to that person.

This scenario happened to me when I was a software engineer. The interviewer had no idea what he was doing. Since he was another engineer, I took the lead. I reviewed my résumé. I talked about projects that I had worked on. I asked some of the questions from my list. I asked if he had questions for me. Instead of being an awkward interview, it turned out quite well. I was asked in for a second interview. The important thing to remember is that you lead the interview from a cooperative perspective. You are not giving commands. If you come across as bossy, egotistical or controlling, you will have lost the interview.

Present your best professional self.

Negativity

I was working on-site with a client and looking to fill a manufacturing engineer position. Mike was a great candidate. My initial phone interview with him went quite well. He had about five applicable years of experience. He was eager to learn and grow. I sent my recommendation to the hiring manager to bring him in for an interview.

Mike came in for the interview. After the interview, I got a message from the manager that he was not interested. I asked why. Mike had spoken negatively about his current co-workers and boss. The manager said that he did not want that kind of negativity and attitude on his team. Clear rejection.

The lesson: Leave the negativity at home.

While in an interview, do not say negative things about any past job, supervisor, peer or company. If you say negative things during the interview, the interviewers will think that you would be the same way if you were to work for them.

This is a great way to get rejected.

Please avoid it. It does not matter whether the statements are true.

In some cases, this can be tough. If you were fired from a job, or if you quit because of a negative work environment, it can be hard to explain the separation without getting negative.

Find a way.

I worked for the-company-that-shall-not-be-named. I was miserable there. The ethics were terrible. I was ordered to lie to a candidate. What did I say when I interviewed for my next position? "I was not comfortable with some of the work practices, so I started to look for a new position. They found out about it and fired me, which is common in the staffing industry, because companies are afraid their clients will get stolen." Was it perfect? No, it still implied some negative things about the company. The second half said something that is common in the staffing industry, so would not really be taken as a negative.

Leave the negative past in the past.

How people get hired

What are the real reasons people get hired?

- Technical (hard skills) competence. For most positions, a significant amount of knowledge or skill is needed. You need to be able to show that you are at least competent, preferably highly skilled. The better your skills come across, the better your chances of landing the job. Odds are good that you have enough strength in this, as shown in your résumé, or you would not have secured an interview. The interview is the place to show people your technical competence.
- Traits or soft skills. For example, communication, relationship building, collaboration, leadership, etc. These are tougher to show and judge from a résumé. The interview is the place to show these. Let your passion for the work show. Use the stories that you have practiced. Examples are the best way to communicate soft skills.

- Ability to build rapport with interviewers. This is one that is not often discussed, and technically could be part of the item above, but is significant, so I am separating it. With several of my clients, I would attend the brief meetings at which the interviewers rated and reviewed candidates. I cannot count how often I heard the phrases "connected with him/her" or "could not connect." It should not be a surprise to know that these impressions with the interviewers carry a lot of weight. Interviewers base the strength of future relationships on the ability to build rapport with a candidate in a very short time. This can make or break an interview for a candidate and has the tough problem of how to provide feedback to a candidate who was unable to do this. The interviewers want to hire someone they feel comfortable with and can work well with but are often at a loss to explain why the interview did not go well.

What can you do to improve yourself in this highly subjective ability?

- Take personal development or communication classes or get involved with a group like Toastmasters.
- Practice interviews with your friends. Or even people whom you do not like, who are more likely to be brutally honest. Get a career coach.
- Put an interests/hobbies section at the bottom of the second page of your résumé. These can be great icebreakers and help to build discussion at the start of an interview.
- Add items to show traits that might not normally be clear in a résumé.

More on rapport

Building rapport with your interviewers is important.

If two people are interviewing for a position and have very similar technical qualifications, the one who does the best job building rapport with the interviewers is the one who will get the job offer.

Many interviewers will start with small talk. This is a way to diffuse tension and begin a conversation and building rapport. The idea is to find commonalities.

Part of the reason I like a Personal Interests section at the end of the résumé is just for this reason. It provides things to talk about that are not related to the job and that could help the interviewer to start conversations and help both people to get comfortable.

Practice mirroring. Pay attention to the speed at which the interviewer is talking. Match the person's speed. Match their body language. This is not manipulation. This is something people do every day in their normal conversations. It is a way to build commonality and rapport.

For example: When I am talking with someone with a French or Southern accent, I naturally start to shift my language patterns in that direction. It is a natural way to ease communication and build rapport. And this explains why most people will eventually lose an accent after moving to a new place. The brain does it naturally.

Do not overdo your mirroring behavior, as that will be taken as mimicry or mocking and as highly negative.

You hope that both you and the interviewer have an interest in the work being done for the job, so that is something you can both talk about with relative ease.

If you can shift the interview into a conversation, by listening and speaking in turn and being relaxed, that is a sign you have done a good job of building rapport.

Tests

Many candidates do not like my opinions on this one.

I feel that almost every interview should include some sort of test.

The format of the test could, and should, vary according to the position. Tests should be directly related to job functions.

In some cases a written test would work, in some cases, an online test. Some tests could be job-related questions in the interview. Some could be solving a problem at a whiteboard. A sales test could involve making some calls.

The point of the interview is to determine your competence at doing the job for which you are interviewing. There should be some way to measure your ability to do the job. In many cases that will be a test.

You can look forward to a test to demonstrate your competence.

Refusal to take a test, for whatever reason, will most likely cause the interviewers to think that you do not have the skills for the job. It may tell them that you have the wrong attitude.

I will qualify here that while I think tests are important, I do not think they should be the only things looked at.

I know one client who used an online test to qualify candidates before they could get an interview. One person did exceedingly well on the test, and they hired that person. They did not have a good in-person interview process and failed to learn some important things about the candidate. The person failed to do the job and had to be fired after three months.

Another client of mine used a test consisting only of three job-related questions. The last one was very difficult to solve. In this case the client did not care about whether the person properly solved the problem but was watching the approach. One candidate refused; she looked at the third question and stormed out of the interview. Clearly a fail. Another failed to solve the problem but showed a good approach and attitude and was hired.

You need to be able to show your competence at doing the job. A test is an opportunity to do this.

What if I do not like it?

A candidate asked: If sometime into the interview process, I realize I do not want to work at this company, should I continue for the practice?

Generally, yes.

If you are treated in a rude, unprofessional or disrespectful manner, and if you see that as a sign of how employees are treated, or if you see other people treated that way during your visit, it would be best to try to politely extricate yourself from the interview. You do not need to work for a company where you will be treated poorly.

But in most cases, it is worth continuing the interview.

- Unless you have a lot of experience interviewing, and most people do not, continue the interview and try your best to interview well, as it is worth the practice. Your extra experience might help you to be better-prepared at the next interview, or you might learn some things about yourself and where you need more practice.
- A negative experience will help you to understand more clearly what you do not want in an employer.
- Completing the interview might get you feedback that you would not get if you were to exit the interview early.
- I had one recent case where a candidate thought the interview was over before he had finished talking with the first person. By the time he had finished talking with the third person (one of the founders of the company), his opinion was reversed. He later accepted an offer from the company. I will not say that this is common, but keeping an open mind can allow new possibilities to unfold.

While I do not think there is perfection in interviewing, I do think practice helps.

Determine cultural fit

How do you determine whether you are a good cultural fit with a company? The first thing to do is to go back to your list of goals, think about which of those are cultural, and make a list of company attributes that are important to you.

Sometimes a company will put a description on their website, or even in a job description, that gives a clear idea of what the company culture is really like.

Usually this is written by marketing and may not really reflect the company culture.

Getting a detailed and accurate idea of a company culture takes some work.

Here are some thoughts:
- Ask a recruiter who does not work for that company, providing you know that you can trust that person, and that they are not just answering out of spite because they cannot get that client.
- Read articles in newspapers and business journals.
- Ask friends and allies who work in the industry.
- See whether you can find a person who had worked there who will talk about it. Again, be aware that this might not be a good source if the job did not end well for that person.
- Job search forums.
- See if you can interview with a peer (detailed in another topic).

Most important is to be observant during the interview.
- Watch people in the corridors. Do people look happy?
- Are there arguments?
- Are all the conference rooms full? Are there a lot of meetings?
- How does the workplace look in terms of organization, colors, neatness?
- Are the restrooms clean?
- How do people treat you? How do they treat each other?
- How are you treated by the person who would be your boss?
- Is there an on-boarding period? Is additional training available?
- Does the company encourage additional education?
- Does the company have a good work/life balance?

Right after the interview, go back to the list of attributes you wanted in a company and check to see whether the company fits it before your memories of the interview fade.

Legal salary discussions

At the time I am writing this, New York State has recently enacted a law making it illegal to ask questions about salary history. Eighteen states now have laws like this, and the number is growing.

I expect most states to have something like this in the next few years. The most common reason for these laws is to reduce the gender compensation gap.

I interviewed a man and a woman for a job. Their ability to do the job was about equal. The woman had slightly more experience than the man. The biggest difference was that the man was asking for 15 percent more on salary. Knowing salary history is not going to change this. In this last case, I advised the woman to increase her expected salary range.

I do not think this law will have the desired effect. In my experience, women tend to be more conservative in what they ask for in their salary requirements.

The point comes back to knowing your worth in the market, regardless of gender. You need to ask for what you are worth, the value you bring to the company.

Part of the problem is that many people still have difficulty talking about salary. I remember when talking about salary was taboo. It was not considered appropriate to talk with my peers or anyone else about my salary. In some companies it was against policy to talk about your salary and could have gotten you fired. It did not take me long working as a recruiter to get over that.

I still see that in others. When I ask people questions about their salary requirements, I am often met with hesitation. Some of this is because of the old taboo; some is because people do not know their own worth in the market.

You need to get comfortable talking about this. Do you know how to do this? I know you get tired of reading this: Practice. When you do practice interviews, include salary discussion.

Better salary discussions

In general, it is better to wait until late in the interview process to talk about salary. You want to have sold yourself before getting into that discussion. Once you have sold the people on your ability to do the job, the salary discussion will be much easier.

Not that you always have a choice. Sometimes the first person you talk with in an interview starts a salary discussion. If that is what happens, you might need to go with it. If it hasn't come up by the end of the interview, you should ask to talk about it then.

My overall take is different from most. (Are you surprised?)

The topic of salary should be a discussion. It should include input from both sides.

You should know your numbers. You should know what you are worth in the market. You should be able to present a target salary range to the person you are speaking with. You also have the right to ask questions. You can ask about the target salary range. You can ask about benefits and bonuses. If your target salary is higher than the company's target range, you can ask whether the company is flexible on that or ask about bonuses.

Having an open discussion is your goal. This has the best odds of ensuring that a mutually agreeable salary range is found.

Despite my initial advice, sometimes it is better to ask the number upfront. Several years ago, I was interested in an HR position at a local college. I looked up the numbers, and it seemed probable that the salary range was less than what my family needed. During my initial phone interview with the college, I honestly expressed my concern and asked for the salary range. It was well under what my family needed. I explained the problem, thanked the person for her time, and asked to be removed from the process.

If you are contacted by an agency about a position, it is in fact common to ask for the salary range upfront, and possibly to provide a target range for the recruiter. This can save everyone a lot of time if the salary range will not work for the position.

I know one person who has a different perspective. It is his belief (based on data from people who do contract negotiation) that it is actually best to be the first person to talk about salary, that the person to talk first has the position of power. It works for him. I do not think it will work for everyone, but I wanted to present it as an option.

Have questions

Possible question to ask:
- What gets rewarded?
- What are the typical day-to-day tasks?
- How are projects planned and scheduled?
- How would you describe the company culture? Is there anything different about the group I would be working with?
- Has this position changed over time? If so, how?

- Why did you come to work for this company?
- What do you like about working for this company?

If you are interested in these things:
- Are there opportunities for advancement?
- What kind of impact does this position have?

What not to ask:
- What does your company do? This is sometimes acceptable at an open job fair. If this is asked during an on-site interview, it is reason for immediate rejection. It tells me that the person has not done any research and has no interest in the job.
- Do not ask too much about what you are getting. It is OK to ask about the benefits package, but do not dwell on it, or other things you might be getting from the job. The interview is primarily to convince them that you can do the job well and help them. I had a candidate rejected because he asked three times about equity during the interview. The time to discuss details of what you are getting is after you have convinced them that you are the right person for the job.

What not to say when they ask if you have questions:
- I do not know.
- I do not think so.

Better answer when they ask if you have questions:
- Thank you. You have already answered all the questions on my list during the interview.

Asking for feedback

Here is another one to try.

No guarantee that this is going to work. I would guess that you have maybe a one-in-three chance of getting some feedback.

The point here is to ask for some feedback before you leave the interview. The odds of getting feedback after the interview are slim, so it might be worth a shot before you leave.

Start by thanking the person for their time or showing appreciation in some other way.

Here are a few possible ways to ask for feedback:
- How do I compare with your ideal candidate?
- Are there any skills that you feel I am lacking to be able to perform the job well?
- Do you have any suggestions to help me be a stronger candidate?

There are two primary reasons for asking for feedback. The first is that you might still be able to address any deficits the interviewer has found with you. The second is to get constructive feedback that may help you in future interviews if you do not get this position.

You are going to find a lot of reluctance to answering your question. Some people want to let HR do it. Some might know that they are going to reject you and do not want to admit it to you. Some might just be uncomfortable with it. Most will not expect it.

Be prepared not to get an answer of substance and be prepared to cheerfully move on.

Ask for what is next

At the end of the interview, you should ask for details about the next steps.

When will they contact you? Who will contact you? In what form can you expect the contact? When should you check in? With whom should you check in?

It is reasonable to know what to expect. This will help you know how to proceed without annoying people.

It may also help you to relax while waiting.

To be blunt, things do not always work as planned. You may not hear from them when expected. You may not hear from them at all. You may just get a rejection letter, or worse, an automated rejection email. And you will probably not get any constructive feedback.

Those things are the realities of a job search. Continue to follow up if you are interested in the position (detailed in a different topic) until you are rejected.

Do not take it personally and do not waste your energy getting angry if things do not happen as explained. Be patient and continue your search.

CHAPTER SIXTEEN: Remote Interviews

Phone interviews

Phone interviews happen before in-person interviews, right? Why put this topic after the Interviews chapter?
- Most of what I told you about interviews also applies to phone interviews.
- Additional interviews by phone happen after an in-person interview.
- Below is what will be different about phone interviews when compared with in-person interviews. Considerations for in-person interviews should still be applied to the phone interview.

What do you need to do to prepare?
- If you are taking the call on a mobile phone, make sure that you are in a place with good reception. Make sure that your phone is fully charged.
- Be in a location where you will not be interrupted by pets, other phone calls, family, etc. Check the location for noise well in advance, e.g., traffic, wind, etc.
- Do not be doing anything else. Keep your focus on the call.

Initial phone interview:
- The main reason for a first interview to be on the phone is efficiency. A call that takes 15 to 30 minutes is much more efficient than three hours. Your résumé will have been reviewed, and they think you are a good fit, but they want to make sure before bringing you in and taking more of the time of the entire team.
- If it is HR calling, it is most likely about the legalities of working, communication or culture.
- If it is the hiring manager calling, or a senior person under the manager, then it is qualifying your ability to do the job.
- Sometimes it is about specific expertise that the team is looking for.

Secondary phone interviews after an in-person interview can be for many reasons:
- They want a person at a remote location to interview you.
- A person who needs to interview you was not available for the in-person interview.
- Clarifying questions. They want to ask more questions about your skill set.
- Differentiation: They are trying to decide between you and another candidate, so need to ask additional questions. They probably will not tell you there is another good candidate.

Video interviews

A new trend is a one-way video interview. As part of the application process, you make a video of yourself answering specific questions that are provided. The person reviewing your application will also review the video.

You do not need to own any special software to do this; it is provided. You may need to give the software permission to use the camera on your device.

Some thoughts:
- If you have a choice of using a phone or a laptop, use the laptop; it will provide a better professional image.
- Dress well. You do not have to be dressed as well as you would for an in-person interview, but it would not hurt.
- Check your background. Make sure there is nothing distracting, no bright lights. A professional setting is best.
- Pick a location with no distractions, interruptions or noise.
- Give yourself adequate time. Do not rush.
- In most cases, you can review the video and record it again.
- Continue the process until you have a recording that you like.

Two-way video interviews are also getting to be more common. They have additional advantages for the company:
- They get a better understanding of you as the candidate, because they can see your body language.
- They can more easily include multiple people in the interview.

Considerations:
- As above, plus
- Be at least 10 minutes early to the interview to resolve possible technical problems, especially if you have not done a video interview before. You may need to install extensions or plug-ins.

CHAPTER SEVENTEEN: Closing the Deal

Changing job descriptions

I was working for a company that did not have anyone working in IT or software development. They wanted to hire their first person to start writing software to automate what they were doing.

I talked with them for a while and helped them to write a job description.

They interviewed a few people. They made changes to the job description.

They interviewed a few more people. They made more changes to the job description.

This was quite frustrating to my candidates, as they were never sure exactly what they were interviewing for. It made it hard on me, too, as it was hard to figure out what candidates to present.

After about three months, they did hire someone.

It is frustrating, but this can happen, for a variety of reasons. It is most frustrating when a job seems to fit you perfectly, and then the new job description has changed away from that.

On rare occasions the job seems to change in a way that is better for the candidate. Or on rare occasions a company finds a candidate they really like and changes the job description to fit that candidate, who may have skills they want but had not originally considered.

Do not let it get to you. If a job description changes, then look at your résumé and make changes to reflect the changes in the job. Or write a résumé addendum. Or send a short letter with a T-chart showing the changes and how you fit the new job. If you have already interviewed, it is worth your time to make those changes, as you are obviously a close enough fit to the original job, or they would not have interviewed you.

Thank-you notes

Do people really expect thank-you letters after interviews?

I cannot tell you how many times people have asked me if they should really write thank-you notes to the people you interviewed with.

No, it is not required. It is not even expected.

Yes, it makes a difference.

An email is good. Handwritten is better (provided that your writing is legible). Typed and mailed is the next best. If you can send an individual note to each person you interview with, that is best, but one message to the team is better than none.

The notes say that you appreciate the time that the people spent with you. They say a lot about your character and what you would be like to work with.

I know a case where two candidates for a job were very closely ranked. One of the two sent thank-you notes. Those made the difference to the hiring team, and that candidate got the offer.

But still most people do not send them.

What should you say?

- Express appreciation for their time.
- Express your interest in the position, even excitement.
- Mention something about the job that you had not known before the interview that got you more interested.
- Mention an item or two about why you are a good fit for the position.
- Tell them that you look forward to the next step.

It does not need to be long. Spend the time to show that the job and people are important to you. It could make the difference and get you the job.

Double-check spelling and grammar.

Follow up, patience

The people you interviewed with are probably busy. Be patient while waiting for a response. If you have sent thank-you notes and have not heard anything back after about a week, it is generally OK to check in with the company.

"It has been a week since my interview with your engineering team. I would like to express again my appreciation for taking the time to talk with me. I am very excited about this position. When can I expect to hear about the next step?"

People also like to know that you are respecting them and appreciating their time. So be respectful and appreciative. Do not get pushy. Patience.

If it has been another week, and you have not heard anything, you should check in again. In addition to being respectful and appreciative, you need to do something a little different. Add value.

"I am looking forward to hearing from you about the Widget Engineer position. Since the interview I have been doing some research on the heat transfer problem that you have been experiencing. I look forward to sharing this research with the team. Thank you again for your time."

Check in with any contacts you have in the company, especially if they include a person who referred you to the position. Do not get pushy. Your contact may not have the ability to find out or get you a status. Sometimes you will get feedback, or your contact's queries will be an indirect cause of your getting feedback from HR.

If more time goes by, and you still have not received a response, it might be time to get more creative.

"I have heard how hard you were all working toward that deadline last week. Enclosed are some chocolate bars to help you recover."

Get creative, but do not go overboard with gifts. A gift that is too expensive will draw negative attention and could even be refused. Pens with your name printed on them (though these can be expensive to make because you might need to buy them in bulk) are OK, as would small pots with potting soil and seeds and a note "for planting creative ideas."

Some companies are fast and some are slow. Either way, patience, persistence, respect and appreciation are your guideline words.

I will add an overriding point here. If, at the end of the interview, you were told what to expect in terms of timing, and told how and when to check in, then you should follow those instructions over my suggestions. Follow the rules that they set down.

Social media checks

It is getting more common, and more controversial, for companies to use social media to review the candidate's public profile before considering an offer.

Stay clean:
- Never write anything negative on any social medium about any company you have worked for. That can be a reason for rejection.
- Keep your private life private as much as possible. If someone you know at a prospective employer is friends with you on Facebook, and can see pictures of you drunk, they might find their way to HR and get you rejected.

If a company asks for your social media account names and passwords:
- Say no. Run.
- You do not want to work for a company that would invade your privacy in that way. If the company wants to see what you wrote that is publicly available, they can do that without your private information.

Limbo

One of the worst things that can happen to you in the course of a job search is to fall into candidate limbo with a company. You interviewed with the company. You thought the interview went well. You sent thank-you notes. You sent follow-up emails. And after weeks, you have heard nothing, not even a rejection letter.

You are probably in candidate limbo.

How can this happen?
- From the company's perspective, you might be a good candidate. Not great enough that they want to hire you immediately. You can do the job, so they did not reject you. Maybe if they search for a few more weeks they will find that great candidate. Maybe they will get an internal transfer whom they do not need to train. Maybe a dozen other reasons. All the indecision causes delay after delay. No one contacts you, until the day the manager decides that the job really needs to be filled, and they finally contact you, only to find that because it has been two months, you have already found another position.

- The manager interviews you then goes on vacation for two weeks. Or travels to some other company sites. When he gets back, the HR representative is on vacation. When the HR rep is back, a big release is coming up, so it is not a good time to start someone new. One delay after another. Hiring is never the priority. They never get back to you until too late.

What can you do? You can maintain contact. Be persistent. Follow up in all the right ways. Sometimes there is nothing you can do. Understand that these things are not your fault, as frustrating as they may be. Keep doing your own part. Odds are pretty good that they will contact you after you have found a new position.

Second chances

Joe interviewed with the company and was thrilled. He thought the interview went great and was excited about the position. The company made the offer to another candidate. The recruiter told him that he was a good candidate, and to keep the door open. A week later, the other candidate rejected the offer, and the company made an offer to Joe.

Do not give up. Sometimes you get a second chance.

After you have been rejected you might be called back.

A manager you interviewed with might recommend you to a manager in a different company.

A manager from a different group within the company might bring you in for a similar position and make you an offer.

All these things and more have happened.

You never know when another door is going to open, because you were talented, respectful, or sent a nice thank-you note.

Getting feedback, Part II

One of the nice things about running my own company is that I can, for the most part, choose the companies that I work with. If a company discriminates or in general makes decisions about candidates for reasons not directly related to their ability to do the job, I can choose not to work with that company. Fortunately, I have not had to do this (fire clients) more than a few times. Usually I get clients via referrals, so I know upfront that they are good companies.

That said, sometimes is it very tough to give feedback. One time it was because the person talked too much at the interview; another had body odor. Another odor reject had not interviewed in years, and his suit smelled like mothballs. Personality mismatches are hard to explain to people also; nothing can be done to help the candidate be better next time.

I know plenty of companies where the automated system (ATS) makes rejecting candidates easy and not very informative. The internal recruiter (or hiring manager) can click one of several legal reasons for the rejection, and a rejection email is automatically sent to the candidate, without attaching the reason. This type of system makes it easier for the recruiter to reject people but also leaves a bad impression of the company, which is also bad in the long term for the company's reputation.

Years ago, I had a six-month on-site contract with a client. Every time we brought candidates for in-person interviews, I would write personalized letters to the candidates who were rejected (I was in the interview review meetings, so I knew all the real reasons that the candidates were rejected). I brought the personalized letters to the VP of engineering who read and signed them (as a contractor, I could not sign a company letter). Candidates were often so happy to receive a personalized letter that they still wanted to work for the company even though they had been rejected.

These are among the reasons recruiters and companies do not give better feedback to candidates:

- Companies are afraid of lawsuits. We live in a society where people can sue over practically anything. Even if a lawsuit is judged frivolous, time and money are spent defending from it. Companies are very concerned about this, even though the frequency of lawsuits related to the interview process is quite low.
- Many people, including those in HR, do not like giving negative feedback. Many people in HR entered that field because they like to help people. It can feel less hurtful to provide someone a generic rejection than to give them actual criticism.
- Lack of communication. Sometimes the hiring manager will send a message to HR to make an offer to a candidate and to reject the rest without any

details about why they are being rejected. Having only information about the best candidate makes it harder to provide feedback to the others.
- The last reason is time. With HR and hiring managers pressed for time, it is much easier to click a button than to think about how to craft a note that will give a person accurate feedback without being offensive. With consistently lower ratios of HR people, and increasing responsibilities, this task often gets dropped.

Dealing with rejection

I know a person who is very careful about the jobs she applies for. She applies, interviews, gets an offer and accepts it. As far as I know, she has never been rejected. This is not normal.

You will get rejections.
- You did not have the skill they were looking for.
- You were not a fit with the team.
- Someone else was better.
- Your salary requirement was too high.
- You have no idea why they rejected you (most common).

Expect it. You will get rejections. Do not let them get you down. Do not publicly be negative about the company. That will never help you.

If you need to get it out, express it privately.

I like to play racquetball. Beating up that little green ball is very therapeutic for me. Do whatever works for you.

Learn from it. Modify your list of goals or career marketing plan if needed.

Move on.

Job offers in writing

Always, always, always get the new job offer in writing before resigning from your current position.

Another recruiter in the agency I was working for had submitted a candidate for a position. The candidate interviewed for the position. The company told the account manager, who told the recruiter, who told the candidate, that they were going to be giving the candidate an offer.

The candidate resigned from his current position.

The client then changed its mind and did not make an offer.

The candidate went back to his employer, which would not allow him to rescind his resignation.

In two weeks, he was unemployed. And he was mad about it. No one had coached him to resign; he did that on his own.

The recruiting team worked hard to find him a new position quickly because he was the primary provider for his family.

The simple solution is that he should not have resigned without the offer letter in hand.

That will not always help. I know another case where a candidate accepted a job and moved to a new state. He walked into his job on the first day and was told that he did not have a job.

There was nothing he could have done differently in this case. I think after some discussion he managed to get some severance pay to allow him to move back to his previous location.

These cases are rare.

Basis for salary

How does a company determine what salary to offer?

The major factors:
- The company's target salary range, which may or may not be up to date with market numbers.
- Perceived value that you bring to the company. This is in technical skills and personality traits. It is shown in previous accomplishments. These are your biggest selling points and are determined by how well you interviewed.
- Perceived value compared with the value of current employees and the salaries they make.
- Candidate's targets

The biggest variable here is the interview. If the interview went great from the company's perspective, then the perceived value is higher. If the interview was just good, then the perceived value is not as high as for the great one.

Your target range tells them what you want, but your interview tells them whether you are worth it. The single biggest thing that you can do is to prepare well for your interview.

Everything else is out of your control.

It is probably not worth trying to figure out the methods the company uses for determining salary. Every company is different. And the hiring manager may have a different perspective also.

Focus on what is in your control.

Low-ball salary companies

Compensation is a big part of any company's expenses, regardless of size or market. There are many companies out there that will do whatever they can to keep salaries down, including making low-ball offers.

How do you avoid getting a low-ball offer?

Your research might give you some hints. Listen for people complaining about pay levels. Look at available sites that show complaints about the company. Review the complaints to see whether any of them are about money. As before, be cautious about how you use the information from these sites.

If you get an interview, pay attention to the culture. Do people look happy? If you get to interview with people who would be your peers, ask whether the company pays market salaries. Listen to the response but also look at the person's reactions.

Have an open discussion about salaries (detailed in another topic). If the company will not have an open discussion about salary, take that as a sign. Do not have high expectations of a company that will not openly discuss compensation with you.

Finally, if you do get a low-ball offer, my suggestion would be to turn it down and run. Stay away from a company that cares more about money than people. Use the offer letter to start a campfire.

Many companies care about their people and pay them market wages. Sometimes it takes time to find them.

If you really need the job, then take it. But make a counteroffer first (yet another topic in this book). Get the best salary that you can. Then work hard at the job, pretend you are happy and keep looking for a better job.

Delay tactics

If you think that you are getting two job offers and want to have both in hand at the same time, you have ways to try to make this work out.

Let us say that you get an offer from Company A. You are expecting an offer from Company B.

Clearly you want to get the offer from Company B before the offer from A expires.

What to do with Company A:
- If you do not have the offer in writing, request it in writing. Of course, you should get the offer in writing anyway.
- Request additional information before the offer expires, e.g., details of their benefits plan. Most often you will need this anyway to understand the total compensation.
- Request additional time to consider the offer. Sometimes if there is significant competition for the position, the company may not want to give you more time, as they have backup candidates. If you are working through an agency, they may not want you to ask for more time. They know that if you are asking for more time, it means you may have another offer, and they might not get their placement. It is still worth asking for additional reasonable time.
- Typically you will not be able to delay the process for more than a week.

What to do with Company B:
- Let them know that you have another offer on the table and are very interested in that offer. And tell them the date by which they would need to provide you an offer and benefits summary.
- Sometimes they will pass, as some companies do not want to rush to put out a job offer, especially if it is a small company. On the other hand, a small company can be more flexible and react more quickly than a larger company.

If you do not hear anything from Company B, do not wait until the last minute to accept the offer from Company A, especially since you would have still needed time to compare the offers. Respond at least a few hours before the end of the workday.

Counteroffers from you

Counteroffers are not just for companies. You can make one yourself.

If you have an offer and are happy with most of it, then you can make a counteroffer to the company and include reasonable changes that you want to the offer. This could include more vacation, a higher salary or flex time, etc.

I would suggest putting this in writing. Email is generally acceptable for this and is considered a legal response for most purposes. While I have seen discussions like this occur on the phone, usually the employer will need time to consider the counteroffer and may need to bring more people into the discussion. Putting it in writing works better.

You can do this even if you are working with an agency, though in that case it may be better to send the request via the agency than to do it yourself. You should talk with the agency about this.

I will add some more qualifiers to this. I do not think it is worth putting in the counteroffer unless you are already strongly considering accepting the offer. Making a counteroffer just to see if you can get the company to offer a higher salary (or whatever you are looking for) is not worth the time of all the people involved if you are not serious about the job.

I would also suggest providing data in support of your request, e.g., if the offer provided you two weeks of vacation, and you have had three for the past 10 years, you can explain that. If the request is about salary, provide market data to support your request.

I also strongly suggest that you offer something in return, e.g., you ask for another week of vacation and tell them that if they grant that, you will accept the offer. Telling the company that you will accept the offer if they grant your changes greatly increases the odds that they will make the better offer.

This does not guarantee that you will be granted the counteroffer. The company may not be able to give you your request. But it puts the request into a different, and more positive, light.

It is OK to say no

Some people find this very difficult to do.
It is OK to decline a job offer:
- If it does not feel right.
- If something in your life has changed, and you cannot accept the position.
- If the overall offer was too low, and they will not or cannot negotiate.
- If it does not fit your goals or career marketing plan.
- You have a better offer.
- Any other reason that is right for you.

What do you do?
- As always, respond in a professional manner.
- If you have been communicating on the phone, it is OK to reject the offer on the phone, but also send a written reply.
- An email response is acceptable.
- Your written rejection should be respectful and appreciative. This company just gave you an offer, and even if you do not want it now, you should leave the company with a good impression of you.
- Thank them for their time and consideration. Give them a reason only if appropriate.
- Finish with as positive a response as possible, as you can never tell what the future might bring or what ripple a positive response might cause.

Reviewing your goals

When I was about to graduate from college, I received two job offers. The first was from a local company making portable telephone switching systems. The second was an out-of-state company working on satellites.

I was having a hard time deciding which offer to accept. I made a list of the attributes of each company and assigned a point value to each. I added them up and the totals of both companies were 111. Yes, identical.

I was a little frustrated, so I took a break and read a book (unrelated to my job search). When I was done, I knew that the out-of-state job would be better for my career. I also knew that I wanted the local job more. I accepted the local position and have been working in this area for more than 30 years.

How do you decide whether a job is the right one? An earlier topic in this book was about looking for your ideal job. You made a list of what you are looking for.

Now you have the offer. Is it what you really want?

Take out the list. Does the current offer have most of those things? Many of those things?

Pay? Benefits? Culture? Purpose? Excitement? Fun products? Social responsibility? Autonomy? Expertise?

How do you decide? What methods do you use to decide? Do you make decisions logically or emotionally? What works for you?

Do you think you would be happy with the new job?

Happy employees are more productive. They get more raises and opportunities, which in turn helps them to be happy employees.

Is this the right job? Is it better than what you have or recently had? Is it what you are looking for?

Deciding and accepting

Read the offer letter in detail. Make sure that you have a copy of the benefits. Take a careful look at everything.

Then go back to your original goals. Make a T-chart comparing your original goals to what is provided by the new offer. Or make more columns if you have more offers.

Does the job meet your goals? Or is it a survival job while you look for the job that you really want?

Make the decision that works best for you, based on your goals and decision-making style.

Accepting the offer is generally simple. Most often you sign the offer letter and send it back to the company. Usually a signed and scanned copy sent via email will work. Most companies do not need the original letter, though some will request that you mail it to them.

A call to HR or the hiring manager, letting them know orally that you are accepting the offer, is appreciated if it will be a while before you can get to a scanner.

Resignation letter

Keep the resignation letter simple.

Do not vent. Do not try to tell the company what they are doing wrong. This is not the time or place.

Stay professional and clear.

In addition to standard addressing include:
- A statement that you are resigning and when you expect your last day to be.
- Express appreciation for your time being employed with the company, even if you do not feel that way. Mention the experience you have gained or things you have learned.
- Optionally you could mention a few of the non-confrontational reasons you are leaving. These should be put in terms of what new things you will be doing in the new position.

Do not:
- Get negative. Vent. Tell them what they are doing wrong.
- Mention your new pay rate or salary. If asked by your manager you can disclose that information orally if you wish to, but you are not required to do so.

Write the letter and meet privately with your direct manager. You can say that you are resigning or just hand the manager the letter.

Set up ways to stay in touch with co-workers and managers whom you have liked working with. If you are not connected with people on LinkedIn, do that soon.

Continue to do your best work right through your last day.

If the company later requests an exit interview, that is the time to talk about the real reasons you are leaving. Try to present them in terms of things that the company could do better. Keep it professional and simple.

Nothing is to be gained by burning bridges. You might possibly want your manager as a reference or you might want to return someday. Stranger things have happened.

Counteroffers from your employer

You have an offer and you just accepted it.

You write your resignation letter and hand it to your manager with a brief discussion.

The next day, the manager calls you into his office with a counteroffer. His offer has a higher salary than the new position you just accepted. What should you do?

In most cases you should turn it down.

In most cases the reason that you are looking for a new position is not just because of money. That might be one of the reasons but is most often not the primary reason.

Better than 95 percent of people who accept counteroffers from their employer end up leaving within one year. More money did not solve the problems.

If the main reason that you are looking for a new position is money, the counteroffer might be worth considering.

If money is not the main reason, look for other things in the counteroffer. Is there anything that will change the other reasons that you were looking? In the rare case that the company makes a counteroffer including immediate changes to your job, then it would be worth considering staying.

But not if the changes are promised for the future. They almost never really happen. And you have a better offer where you will get those changes now; why should you wait six months or a year?

I hope you looked into solutions to solve your problems with the current position before you started to look for a new one.

There are other reasons not to accept the counteroffer. Your manager and co-workers may always be wondering when you are going to leave. Some may feel you have broken their trust. You may get passed by for possible promotions or interesting projects. Whatever your reasons were before, they will likely get stronger.

Exit interviews

A friend asked me about doing an exit interview. He had just accepted a new position and was asked to do the interview by HR. He had heard that it was mostly not worth doing. He did not agree with that, and I do not either. I think it is worth doing and I have these points to make:

- Do not burn any bridges. Do not throw people under the bus. Being negative is not going to help. First, it will not help the company to improve. Second, the company will not want you back. Most people think that they would never want to return to a job they quit, but I have seen a surprising number of people go back to a company that they had been working for previously. Sometimes leaving and going to a new place makes people realize what they had. Or maybe the new job is not nearly everything that was promised. Whatever the reason, leaving with a lot of negatives is not going to help you or the company or the people you worked with.
- Leave feedback. This is where many people disagree with me. In many cases, the information learned by HR in the exit interview does not make any difference to the company. I think that it is still worth leaving feedback. Sometimes a company does change and improve. Sometimes the feedback is useful. While it is true that most often your feedback will not be used, I think that it is worth giving because maybe this will be one of those times when it will help. I think it is worth your time. Maybe it will help the people who were your co-workers. Maybe it will help the company be better, in case you go back to it someday.

CHAPTER EIGHTEEN: A New Beginning

Starting a new job

While this book is about helping you to find a job you love, my hope is that you will do well at the new position once you have found it, and not be looking for a job again soon after. When you get done with the piles of new-hire paperwork here are a few considerations:

- Observe. Look to see if what you saw during your interview is the way that things really are.
- Look for allies. You may already have some, people whom you knew before you applied, or people from the interview process, but it is always worth making new alliances.
- Pecking order. Pay attention to the existing hierarchies. Watch people who are effective and observe how they get things done.
- Ask questions. Be a sponge. The more you learn about how the company works, the more efficient and effective you can be.
- Set some goals. Ask your new boss for short- and long-term goals, but also set your own personal goals. What do you want to achieve? What do you want out of your new position?

Forward networking

Do not stop networking once you have found a position. The reasons:

- What people miss most when they leave a job is the people. Stay connected with those people. Continue to build your relationships.
- I have seen people exit their job search networks once they have found a job. It makes me wonder what they learned from being part of those groups. Please do not be one of those people.
- The single best way for people to find jobs is through their network. That means you. When you have

found that job you love, it is likely that you had a lot of help from people in your network. Pay it forward. Be there for others. Probably not the people who helped you directly, but that does not matter. Be part of a network of people who help each other. Make time to help others who are looking for something better.
- You likely learned a lot during your job search, and your insights could help another person move forward. Or many people. Allow your wisdom to help people.
- Someday you may need your network again. Be part of a community of people who help each other to find the best possible job.

It is worth it to keep up your network, to stay involved. Building your network can have unrelated benefits. While interviewing a candidate, I learned that he had done foster care. Later he was able to answer several questions I had about how things really worked in the foster care system. This is not related to a job search but is related to the point of keeping up your network. You never know where it could help.

If it does not work out

John started his new position. One week after he started, there was a reorganization, and he was moved to a different group. He was now working on a project that did not interest him and where his skills did not apply.

Or your boss resigns and leaves. Or the company is bought by a larger company. Things can go wrong.

What do you do?

- Put in 100 percent. It is still your career. Even if you hate the changes, you can persevere and put in your best for a while.
- Look for positive change. Talk with your boss or HR to see what can be done to fix the problems. Stay positive and professional. If you are angry or confrontational, you will not make headway.
- If those things fail, restart your job search.

- If you go to an interview, explain the problem in a positive way. "As soon as the job started, I was switched to a position that does not allow me to use my strengths."
- If you leave soon after starting, you may need to pay back any training fees or signing bonuses.

Keep a résumé ready

It is good to keep your résumé ready, because you never know what could happen. The company you are working for might suddenly have some layoffs. An old friend might call with your dream job. Factors good or bad might happen for which you might need a résumé.

Another reason is also important. If you regularly update your résumé you can add in projects that you are working on while they are fresh in your mind, and while you know the achievements.

Many times, I have interviewed candidates and asked about their achievements on a job, only to find that they could not remember. Sometimes they had no documentation of the work they did to help them remember.

The first time I got laid off, I was well-set with documentation. While in the job, I had written weekly reports to my supervisor on the work I was doing. I had summarized these into a report for the annual review. I had kept the reports and the performance-appraisal document, so I had a ready supply of information for my résumé when I received my layoff notice.

I am not suggesting that you update your résumé every time you finish a project, but that if you update it a few times a year, or keep documents that show what you have worked on, you will be able to have a timely account of the projects you worked on.

Keeping up with the job market

Before I was self-employed, I had a tough time keeping up with the job market. I had my job and my hobbies, and I did not really think about changing jobs.

Some things annoyed me about my first job. Then I was called by a headhunter. I interviewed and accepted the new job before I thought about what my long-term goals would be.

I was laid off from both my second and third jobs. In theory, I should have been aware that both of those were coming. In both cases, corporate financial problems might have been visible. I did not think too much about it. To be fair, if it was not my job to stay on top of the job market; I still might not be good at it today. I suspect a lot of people like myself are out there, who just do not often think about the next job.

My suggestion would be to look at the job market at least once a year. You do not have to apply for jobs, just look at it to see what's around. Update your career marketing plan if necessary.

Look at hiring trends. Go to a salary checker to see whether you are getting paid at the market rate. Look at possible changes happening in your profession. It is OK to apply for jobs that look interesting. It is OK to listen if someone wants to hire you away from your current job. There is no right or wrong about how often to apply for positions or go on interviews. Some people like to stay with a job for a long time. Others like to change more frequently. Be aware of trends in your own profession.

The most important thing is to keep your goals in front of you to guide you if you start actively looking.

CHAPTER NINETEEN: Coronavirus Update

SARS-CoV-2, Covid-19, Coronavirus

The Novel Coronavirus, also known as SARS-CoV-2 and Covid-19, is causing massive changes in the working world. If you are unemployed, your job search just got a lot harder. If you are employed and looking, you probably put your search on hold, because most of the companies you were talking with probably put their jobs on hold.

Some companies will entirely change the way that they work, some will go back to the way it was once. Some will adapt; others will fall back on what is known and comfortable once this is past.

Most of the information in this book will still be true, but not for all employers. We do not know what will change and what will not.

An example: I have heard people saying (and writing) that we will never go back to shaking hands again. I have heard others say that once this is over, you can expect to be shaking hands at interviews and networking events. Only time will tell what will happen.

Pay attention. Adapt.

What to do differently

Here are some suggestions for adapting:
- Stay safe. Follow government guidelines.
- Pay attention to the market, especially in your own profession. Some professions and industries will be growing; others will take massive losses. If you are in a market that is losing ground, start to consider new options.
- If you are having trouble adapting mentally or emotionally, free mental health services are available in many states.

Working from home:
- If you work in an office, and have not already done so, create a home office space. If you do not have a

room that you can use as an office, try to find a quiet space where you can work and not be disturbed.
- Get a headset with a microphone. This will cut out surrounding noise for you when you are on a call or in a meeting and will give better quality and reduce noise for others.
- Find ways to stay physically active. Telecommuting is less physically active. Find an activity to maintain your health. The number of laps from your refrigerator to your desk does not count.

Personal development:
- Build your contacts. Check in with people on your contact list to see how they are doing. Connect with new people on LinkedIn. Search previous employers for people you know whom you can connect with.
- Keep your career marketing plan updated.
- Develop new skills. Lots of online training courses are now available at huge discounts.

If you are unemployed:
- Expect that finding a new position will take longer. Consider temporary local or virtual positions to help pay the bills, even if they are not in your chosen field.

If you are employed and looking for a new position:
- You may want to hold off for a while.
- Maybe the job you are in will get better. Maybe you will not want to leave. Change is in the air. Maybe you can foster changes to make it into the job you want.
- Over the next few months, companies will grow and companies will fail. Watch the companies in your career marketing plan. Pay attention to how they are doing. You do not want to jump into a company that is about to do layoffs.
- Stay in touch with companies with which you may have been interviewing before the shutdown. If a company is hiring, odds are good that they will come through the pandemic well.

- I understand that these points may seem contradictory. Anything is possible, so the point is to be observant, so you keep aware of which way the changes are going.

Hiring process changes

What changes can you expect?
- Expect constant changes in the job market for the next two years. Layoffs and hiring will be erratic.
- Phone interviews will be more common, regardless of whether companies did them before.
- Video interviews will become much more common (see the Topic on Video Interviews).

What can you do?
- Keep looking. Some companies will be hiring.
- Stay in touch with people from previous opportunities. Jobs may reopen.
- Watch how your target companies respond to the pandemic.
- Practice remote interviewing, both phone and video.
- Continue your standard interview research.

New interview questions to ask:
- How has the Coronavirus affected your company?
- How has the Coronavirus affected work processes? Is there more remote working? Do you expect that to continue?

In-person interview expectations:
- You can expect companies to provide you with protocols to reduce virus spread at the interview. If you do not get this, you should ask. This may include asking you not to shake hands with people.
- You can expect social distancing. The use of masks, gloves, hand sanitizers and other procedures will vary by company.
- Always stay safe. If you think that the company is not following proper safety standards you have the right to leave.

Work changes

Rich was excited. To get quotes to his clients, he had to tour the company's warehouse. But the Coronavirus lockdown had been preventing him from traveling. A client suggested a walk-though via a phone app. His client walked him through, and Rich got a quote sent out to the client the next day. No need to travel. It has also been easier to find a time when the client could meet with him. His life has changed, and for the better.

There is no way to know what changes are in store for us because of the Coronavirus.

You can expect more innovations in work-from-home methods and ways to improve remote working.

You can expect some companies to try to go back to the way things were. Companies that did not allow remote work, but that shifted to remote work out of need, may want to go back to having everyone at the office. You can expect passionate discussions.

Some companies will embrace the change and become better for it.

Some companies will go under or get smaller to survive.

As individuals, many of us have been forced to embrace changes. For some it has made life better, for some harder. But we are learning from this. It is certain to change our lives.

CHAPTER TWENTY: The End

Thank you

Writing this book has been an adventure for me. I have learned quite a bit. In writing and researching I have found that some of my opinions have changed. I have modified some of the advice that I give people.

This book has changed my life in positive ways. I hope that the content of this book has, or will, help you make positive, happy and healthful changes to your work and life.

Blessings on your journey.

www.ingramcontent.com/pod-product-compliance
Lightning Source LLC
LaVergne TN
LVHW020929090426
835512LV00020B/3273